A Dictionary of
Terms and Techniques in

Archaeology

Sara Champion

Facts On File, Inc.
119 West 57th Street, New York, N.Y. 10019

CC70
C46

Phaidon Press Limited
Littlegate House, St Ebbe's Street, Oxford

Published in the United States of America by
Facts on File, Inc., New York
119 West 57th Street, New York, N.Y. 10019

This edition first published 1980
© 1980 by Phaidon Press Limited

ISBN 0–87196–445–7
Library of Congress Catalog Card Number: 80–66774

Designed by Richard Garratt
Printed and bound in Great Britain by
Morrison and Gibb Ltd, London and Edinburgh.

Photographic Acknowledgements

p. 6 (upper): Cambridge University Collection: copyright reserved. *p.* 6 (lower): Aerofilms Ltd. *p.* 9: M3 Archaeological Rescue Committee. *p.* 10: Faunal Remains Project, Southampton University. *p.* 13 (upper): Musée Miln. *p.* 13 (lower): University of London, Warburg Institute. *p.* 15: Courtesy of Dr. K. A. Barber. *p.* 16: Courtesy of US Forest Service. *p.* 18: Royal Commission on Historic Monuments (England): Crown copyright. *p.* 23: Courtesy of Trustees of the British Museum, Oxford. *p.* 26: Courtesy of P. Clayton. *p.* 27: Ashmolean Museum, Oxford. *p.* 30: Courtesy of N. Bradford. *p.* 32: Courtesy *Studies in Conservation*. *p.* 33: Wilts. County Council Library and Museum Service. *p.* 35: Courtesy of the Laboratory of Tree-Ring Research, University of Arizona. *p.* 36: Courtesy of Dr. P. A. Holdway. *p.* 37: Northants Development Corporation. *p.* 38: Courtesy of Prof. A. C. Renfrew. *p.* 44 (upper): Society of Antiquaries of London. *p.* 44 (lower): Courtesy of Dr. T. C. Champion. *pp.* 45, 46: Butser Ancient Farm Project Trust. *p.* 49: General Electric Research and Development Centre, New York. *p.* 54: Cambridge University Collection: copyright reserved. *p.* 55: University Museum of Archaeology and Ethnology, Cambridge. *p.* 56: Courtesy of Trustees of the British Museum. *p.* 61: Courtesy of N. Bradford. *p.* 64: National Museum of Ireland, Dublin. *p.* 65: Courtesy of H. Kenward. *p.* 74: Courtesy of C. Caple. *p.* 75: Courtesy of N. Bradford. *p.* 79: Devizes Museum, Wiltshire. *p.* 80: Courtesy of British Museum (Natural History). *p.* 82: Courtesy of Irving Friedman, U.S. Geological Survey, Denver, Colorado. *p.* 84: Courtesy of Dr. H. W. Catling. *p.* 86: Courtesy of Dr. P. Mellars. *p.* 90: Courtesy of P. Clayton. *p.* 92: Courtesy of Dr. N. Hamilton. *p.* 94: Courtesy of Dr. D. Williams. *p.* 97: Courtesy of Prof. G. W. Dimbleby. *p.* 98: Courtesy of R. Bradley; photo, R. J. Francis. *p.* 99: Musée du Louvre. *p.* 102: Courtesy of N. Hartmann, MASCA. *p.* 106: Courtesy of Prof. J. A. Steers. *p.* 115: Courtesy of R. Shepherd. *p.* 117: Courtesy of Biologisch-Archaeologisch Institut, Gröningen. *p.* 119: Courtesy of P. Clayton. *p.* 126: Society of Antiquaries of London. *p.* 128: Ashmolean Museum, Oxford. *p.* 131: Courtesy of Dr. S. J. Fleming. *p.* 135: Ashmolean Museum, Oxford. *p.* 136: Courtesy of Royal College of Surgeons. *p.* 139: Courtesy of Geological Survey of Finland.

Introduction

This dictionary has been compiled with the aim of introducing to non-professional archaeologists the terms and techniques used in modern archaeology. Any interested amateur may now pick up an excavation report or an archaeological volume and be faced with terms like 'locational analysis', 'ceramic petrology' or 'X-ray fluorescence spectrometry', and not know what the technique is attempting to achieve, nor the methods by which it is carried out. Archaeology has changed dramatically in the last thirty years, at first through the development of new dating techniques, for example radiocarbon dating, and more recently through the borrowing and adaptation of a whole series of new techniques from other disciplines: from anthropology, biology, botany, chemistry, computer studies, demography, economics, geography, geology, mathematics, pathology, physics, statistics and surveying. It is hardly possible for any person to be an expert in all these fields, but it is necessary for anyone interested in modern archaeology to understand the terminology and the basic aims of the techniques.

The dictionary is not a general dictionary of archaeology: names of cultures and artefacts have been deliberately omitted. In general, terms have been included if they describe a technique applied to archaeological material either in the past or as part of modern analysis. Theoretically, therefore, the techniques described are applicable to suitable material throughout the world, and those terms derived from prehistoric technology are also universal. It has, even so, been difficult to decide on omission or inclusion in cases where technical terms are used only locally. There are also likely to be some omissions through my own lack of knowledge. There are certainly judgements implicit in some entries which are my own, or which appear as a reflection of received opinion in Britain, with which readers may well disagree.

Archaeology continues to develop at a very fast rate: even during the writing of the book further improvements in the radiocarbon dating technique were announced, and the widespread interest in many scientific techniques will undoubtedly lead to further refinements. Continuing research may well result in a reduction in the apparent reliability of some techniques suggested by preliminary results. Similarly, locational models borrowed from geography, and mathematical models of human societies and cultural development, are areas of active, current interest. In view of the disenchantment beginning to be felt in some of the other disciplines from which these techniques have been borrowed, it will be interesting to see how successful is their application to archaeology.

I am not an expert in most of the techniques described, and have not attempted to explain the physical, mathematical or chemical theory behind them. I felt it essential, therefore, to provide a reference for many of the techniques so that more detail could be sought from suitable sources. In order not to overload the text with bibliographical references, these have been restricted in general to one per entry. A general bibliography is also included at the end.

I would like to conclude by stating that I have benefited greatly from the writings of all those archaeologists and scientists from whose works this dictionary has been distilled: they will doubtless recognize their contribution. I have also valued greatly discussions with colleagues, especially those in Southampton. A special mention is due to Jane Timby, who helped so much with the choice of illustrative material, and to my husband, Tim Champion, who wrote some of the entries and with whom I discussed many others.

Absolute dating

Techniques of dating which result in dates given in terms of the calendar, that is, in years before present or B.P. A more recent term for this type of dating is chronometric dating (q.v.).

Activity area

A term used in American archaeology to describe the smallest observable component of a settlement site, an area where an activity of some nature took place.

Adobe

Mud bricks which have not been fired but which are hardened and dried in the sun. Though really suitable only for sunny climates, this building material has on occasion been used in antiquity in wetter areas, with predictable results.

Aerial photography

One of the most important techniques used in archaeology, since it can provide detailed information about sites and their relationship to the landscape without excavation. It has proved to be of crucial importance since the widespread destruction of the landscape through road-building and modern agricultural practices, because new sites have in many cases been located before destruction has started. It was first realized that an aerial view could show previously unrecognized details of the landscape when ballooning became popular, and the increase of aeroplane flights during the two World Wars was a spur to further development of the technique.

There are three ways in which sites can be recognized from the air. Probably the most familiar is the crop-mark phenomenon. Marks of sites appear in sympathetic crops, such as cereals, because features which are dug into the ground—pits, ditches and gullies—are often filled with looser, more water-retentive material than the surrounding soil, often organic in nature; therefore the crop grows taller and greener in these areas. In places where stony banks or stone walls have left their foundations, the crops cannot root so deep, nor find as much water, and they tend to be shorter and to ripen yellow earlier. Thus a plan of the site, ditches, walls and pits, can be reflected in the crop. The same site will not be susceptible every year to aerial photographs, as local climatic variation affects the nature of the feature fillings; a site may only be seen once in ten or twenty years. There are also some regions where crop-marks never show due to local geological factors.

The second way in which sites are recognized is through soil-marks. These may also be observed on the ground, but may only make a sensible pattern from the air. Where a large feature is filled with dark, carbon-flecked occupation soil, it may show clearly against a lighter topsoil, particularly immediately after ploughing. Similarly, stone walls will frequently leave fragments of broken stone near the surface where they can be picked up by the plough: complete building plans can be located in this way.

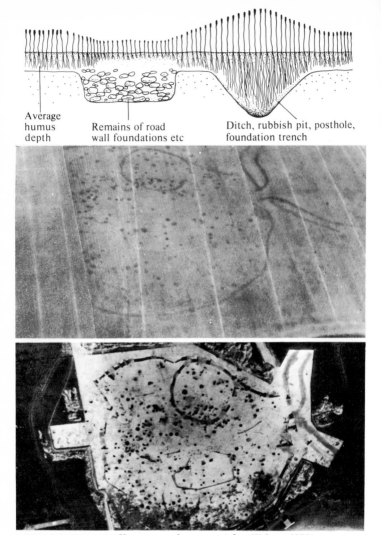

Average humus depth

Remains of road wall foundations etc

Ditch, rubbish pit, posthole, foundation trench

AERIAL PHOTOGRAPHY *How cropmarks appear (*after *Webster 1971).*
Iron Age settlement at Gussage All Saints, Dorset, England. Centre *Air*
photograph showing cropmarks visible before excavation (note the absence of
marks on the left caused by a change in the crop). Below *The site from the air*
during excavation, showing the accuracy of the pre-excavation photograph in
pinpointing features.

The third manner in which features are revealed is by shadow-marks. Oblique views of the landscape in early morning or late evening sun, when shadows are long, reveal shallow banks or humps which may be the last remains of originally more substantial structures. Though these can sometimes be recognized on the ground by careful fieldwalking and contour planning, much larger areas can be examined from the air, and overall patterns will be clearer. Those who study aerial photographs can recognize different types of site and feature, and detailed interpretations of photographs are now available. The use of false-colour infra-red photography (q.v.) has increased the versatility of aerial photography in recent years, while the development of photogrammetry (q.v.) allows the accurate mapping of both archaeological and geographical information. An extension of the technique to involve the use of satellites is not unlikely if problems of detail can be resolved.

Ref.: DEUEL, L. *Flights into Yesterday*. London, 1969.

Aerobic
An environmental state in which oxygen is present and which, therefore, causes decay to take place in organic structures. In aerobic conditions plants, timber, leather, flesh, food remains and clothing will disintegrate.

Alidade
A device used in surveying and planning with a plane-table (q.v.). It consists of a telescopic sight with stadia hairs mounted on a graduated metal ruler. It incorporates a prismatic eyepiece and a spirit level for levelling the plane-table; some also include compasses, and most modern instruments can measure angles up to 30°.

Alluvium
Material deposited by rivers. Though the largest areas of alluvium are flood plains and deltas, build-up of alluvial material may occur where a river overflows its banks. It is very fertile soil consisting of gravel, sand, silt and clay as well as organic material, and therefore provided an attractive environment for early farmers.

Amino-acid dating
A relatively new technique of chronometric dating which it is hoped may fill the gap between dates that can be established by radiocarbon dating (q.v.) and by potassium-argon dating (q.v.). The basis for the technique is the fact that almost all amino-acids, which are present in living organisms, racemize, that is they change from optically active to optically passive compounds, over a period of time. Careful choice of a particular amino-acid, such as aspartic acid, with a suitable half-life of 15,000 to 20,000 years should allow dates from 5,000 to 100,000 years to be calculated. However, racemization is a process very much affected by environmental factors such as temperature change: if there has been any significant alteration in temperature during the period in which the object has been buried, large errors may result. Various different problems of contamination have also arisen, so that the technique can in no way be said to be established. Material that has been dated so far includes fossil bones

7

and deep-sea sediments, the latter presenting fewer problems since temperature has been generally more stable.

Ref.: BADA, J. L. and PROTSCH, R. 'Racemization reaction of aspartic acid and its use in dating fossil bones', *Proc. Nat. Acad. Sciences* 70 (1973), 1331–4.

Anaerobic
This term, the opposite of aerobic (q.v.), describes an environmental situation where oxygen is excluded and where, therefore, decay of organic material is halted partially or completely. In anaerobic conditions, which are usually waterlogged but which may be, for example, sealed under an impervious layer of clay, plant and animal remains will survive to a much greater extent than normal.

Annealing
This is one of the most important stages in metalworking. After casting the metal, it may be necessary to further process the object by cold-working, hammering and drawing the metal either to produce hard cutting edges or to produce beaten sheet metal. Hammering makes the metal harder, though increasingly more brittle, and since it actually destroys the crystalline structure, it can eventually crack the metal. Annealing, the reheating of the metal gently to a dull red heat and allowing it to cool, produces a new crystalline structure which can be hammered again. The process may be repeated as often as is necessary. The final edge on a weapon may be left unannealed as it is harder and more lasting that way.

Antimonial bronze
As with arsenical bronze (q.v.), the antimony present as a third constituent in antimonial bronze may well have been deliberately sought after in the original copper ore used in the alloy, since it improves the hardening qualities.

Archaeobotany
The study of botanical remains from archaeological sites. While palaeobotany (q.v.) includes the study of non-archaeological material, and palaeoethnobotany (q.v.) includes strictly the flora specifically connected with man, archaeobotany can be seen to be the study of both the natural surroundings and the anthropogenically controlled species of a site. All these terms are used interchangeably in archaeological literature.

Archaeomagnetic intensity dating *see* MAGNETIC DATING

Archeomagnetism *see* MAGNETIC DATING

Archaeozoology
The study of animal bones from archaeological contexts. It involves all the processes from the collection, cleaning, sorting, identification and measurement of bones to the study and interpretation of the results.

A variety of different questions may be asked of a collection of animal bones, and the answers may throw a great deal of light on the environment and subsistence economy of the associated human settlement. The bones are collected from the site in the same way as other finds, and are examined in a laboratory after washing and any necessary conservation. Since collection tends to favour the bones of larger species, as they survive in larger pieces, it is important to ensure a balanced sample by implementing careful recovery procedures. The subsequent recording of the bones is carried out to varying standards depending on facilities available as well as expertise. The minimum acceptable is to record visible details and to undertake overall measurement, but some laboratories now employ a sophisticated system of measurement which allows a much more detailed study of the material. Naturally, during recording, species will be identified and notes will be made on dentition (q.v.). Study of the bones involves calculations of minimum numbers of individuals belonging to each species found, size, age, sex, stature, and whether the bones have any marks from implements implying butchering and eating. The sort of questions that might be asked are: how many species of domesticated animals are there (the answer could suggest the degree of farming specialization); how far are wild animals exploited; are there groups of animal bones from very young age groups (the answer would suggest kill patterns related to inability to maintain full herds over the winter); in what way were the bones butchered; are the sex ratios unusual (the answer could suggest breeding strategies); and are any animals unusual in size.

By analysing remains from different parts of the site it may be possible to understand some of the internal organization of the settlement—to define areas of butchering, cooking and boneworking—while a com-

ARCHAEOZOOLOGY *Articulated horse skeleton found in a rubbish pit on a site at Winnall Down, Hampshire, England.*

ARCHAEOZOOLOGY *Above The semi-automatic bone-measuring and recording equipment in use at the Faunal Remains Unit, University of Southampton. It comprises electronic callipers with digital display, an interface unit, and a teletype which produces punched tape for computer recording. Below An example of the results of the analysis of animal bones. These histograms show the increasing distal width in mm. of the tibiae of sheep/goat at Exeter, Devon, from the medieval period to AD 1600. (Courtesy of J. M. Maltby).*

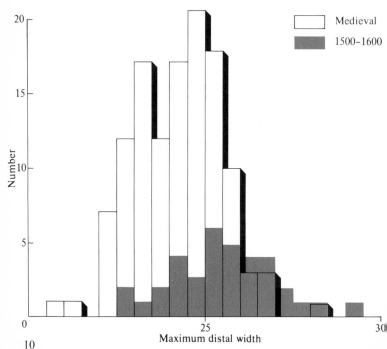

parison between sites within a region may show areas of specialization. Certain particular fields of study have developed: one is concerned with the earliest stages of animal domestication, where detailed study of the morphology of the animal bones can show differences between the wild forebears and early domesticates due to care and special breeding. Though the field is well-established and the potential understood, there are still few places in the world where facilities are adequate for processing animal bones from the hundreds of sites excavated every year.

Ref.: CHAPLIN, R. E. *The Study of Animal Bones from Archaeological Sites.* London, 1971.

Area excavation
A method of excavation where large areas are open at any one time; also known as extensive excavation. The horizontal plan and relationship between features are considered to be as important as the vertical stratigraphy, which on a site of this nature is frequently non-existent.

Arsenical bronze
Bronze (copper and tin) which contains a third constituent, arsenic, in small proportions (about 2–3%). While in the case of bronze containing a lower percentage of arsenic it is thought that the inclusion is insignificant, it is probable that for the objects with up to 3% arsenic the ore was especially chosen for its arsenical content, since it has a hardening effect on the final alloy.

Artefact (or artifact)
Any object that has been made, modified or used by man. It may range from a coarse stone used in the manufacture of flint to anything of high technical accomplishment in any material.

Articulation
The state of bones when they lie in the relationship to each other that they had in life. If a skeleton is articulated, it is assumed that it reached its final resting place while there were still ligaments and flesh to hold it together.

Assemblage
A set of objects found in association with each other and therefore assumed to belong to one phase and one group of people. An assemblage can be made up of objects of different type, for example pottery, flint or metal tools, unlike an industry (q.v.) which describes a set of objects in one medium. An assemblage may reflect the totality of artefacts available to a particular group of people at one time; the same assemblage found at other sites may suggest the existence of a culture (q.v.).

Association
Objects are said to be in association with each other when they are found together in a context which suggests simultaneous deposition. The objects found in a grave will be associated, as will those found close together in a single layer in a pit. Associations between objects are the basis for relative

dating or chronology (q.v.) and the concept of cross-dating. If pottery and flint tools were never associated in a closed context there would be few, if any, grounds for linking them into an assemblage (q.v.), and the full material culture of any group would not be available. The association of undated objects with artefacts of known date allows the one to be dated by the other.

Atomic absorption spectrometry

One of the physical methods of analysis used to determine the chemical composition of metals, such as copper, and non-metallic substances such as flint. It is not a completely non-destructive technique, since a small sample must be removed from the artefact (between 10mg. and 1g. depending on the concentration of the elements). The sample is first taken into solution, and is then atomized in a flame; focussed on this is a light, provided by a hollow cathode lamp made from, or lined with, the element to be analysed. The light thus has a defined wavelength corresponding to the emission wavelength of the chosen element. The atoms of that element in the sample therefore absorb a proportion of the light, measured with a photomultiplier, and a comparison of the intensity of the light with that which has not gone through the sample shows the extent of the absorption, thus providing an estimate of the amount of the chosen element in the specimen. One of the drawbacks in the use of the method is that a separate measurement (and a different hollow cathode lamp) is necessary for each element, so that analysis for a large number of elements is time-consuming. There are also problems of contamination with the high dilutions necessary for elements present in high concentrations, so that the method is used for the analysis of minor elements and trace elements rather than for major elements. On the other hand, the results are generally more accurate than those obtained using optical emission spectrometry (q.v.), so that the technique will probably be used increas-

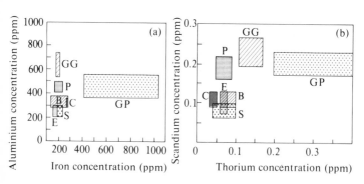

ATOMIC ABSORPTION SPECTROMETRY *Concentrations of two elements in flint revealed by atomic absorption spectrometry, showing the differences between flint from Grand Pressigny (GP), Britanny, and that from other sources (*after *Sieveking* et al *1970).*

A dagger of Grand Pressigny flint from near the Saint-Michel barrow, Carnac, Brittany. Length 14 cm.

ingly, particularly for the identification of sources of metal ores through the recognition and quantification of the trace elements.

Ref.: TITE, M. S. *Methods of Physical Examination in Archaeology.* London, 1972, 264–6.

Auger

A tool used to probe levels below the ground in order to extract information without excavating. Used in a wider context for geological, mining and other work, its most useful applications in archaeology are first as a means of sampling and understanding the geological environment of a site, and secondly for the extraction of peat or other cores for the purpose of pollen analysis (q.v.). Various types of auger are available—a version with a screw-like thread is frequently used for geological work, while for the extraction of cores for pollen analysis a hole may be drilled first and then an auger introduced which removes a column of material.

Barbotine

A technique of pottery decoration involving the application of a slip (q.v.) to the pot, not in an even layer but in the form of thick incrustations in

A pot decorated in the BARBOTINE *technique from Verulamium, Hertfordshire, England. 2nd–3rd century* AD. *Height 22.5 cm.*

patches or trails. In certain types of pottery the barbotine decoration may form a picture or a pattern.

Bar chart

A method of representing quantified data frequently used by archaeologists. Each bar represents a count of units: an assemblage of eleven different types of flint tool can be represented with eleven bars on the horizontal scale, the actual numbers or percentage of the total of each type being recorded on a vertical scale. The bar chart gives an immediate visual representation of the components of the assemblage. The order in which the different units are listed can be arbitrary, since the units measured are discrete. There is some confusion, because of the visual similarity, between a bar chart and a histogram (q.v.), though the latter represents different measurements of the same attribute and therefore the horizontal scale is not arbitrary but ordered. The use of bar charts to compare assemblages may require the superposition of one on another, which makes the picture unclear even if the rectangular bars are replaced by points which may be joined by a line. The convention of 'cumulative bar charts' has been developed to deal with this problem: the values of succeeding bars are added to the previous ones, creating a cumulative graph. These are useful for comparative purposes, but are difficult to break down into their individual units.

Baulk

A section of earth left standing between trenches on an excavation, and also the edges of a large area excavation. The baulk provides a constant reference to the original pre-excavation level of the site, and also carries all sections along or across the site. In an excavation carried out according to the grid method (q.v.), 25% of the site may consist of baulks, and frequently the answer to problems of stratigraphy or interpretation may lie underneath them.

Beta-ray backscattering

A non-destructive physical method of chemical analysis which, though limited in its application, has been used successfully to determine the lead content of glass and glaze. The specimen is subjected to a beam of electrons from a weak radioactive beta source; some electrons are absorbed, while others are backscattered from the surface of the sample, and can be counted with a Geiger counter. The percentage of electrons backscattered is dependent on the atomic number of the elements constituting the surface layer of the artefact, and therefore if an element with a high atomic number is known to be present (lead, for instance), an estimate can be gained of its concentration. There are several limitations to this technique: the element responsible for the backscattering must be known before analysis, since the equipment cannot distinguish between high concentrations of elements with medium atomic numbers and low concentrations of elements with high atomic numbers. The equipment cannot sense very small amounts of an element, and factors such as the thickness of a glaze affect the amount of backscattering. An advantage is the cheapness and portability of the equipment, and it can therefore be a useful technique for analysing material like glass where basic differences in technology are under investigation.

Ref.: EMELEUS, V. M. 'Beta-ray backscattering: a simple method for the quantitative determination of lead oxide in glass, glaze and pottery', *Archaeometry* 3 (1960), 5–9.

Biome
A word used to describe an ecological community of plants and animals established over a wide area: for example, the oak/deer biome, or the spruce/moose biome of North America.

Bivalve mould
This term refers to a mould for casting metal objects which is more complicated than an open mould (q.v.). Two halves of a mould of stone, clay or metal are pegged together, the space between them having the shape of the object being·cast. After the metal has cooled, the mould is opened and can be re-used.

Blanket peat
Ombrogenous peat which forms in areas where rainfall is high, since it derives almost all its moisture from the atmosphere. As it is not dependent on ground water, like topogenous peat (q.v.), it can form on higher ground like plateaux; in periods of climatic change it can alter its nature, developing tree cover in drier periods and then recurring as a bog when rainfall increases. In a peat bog of this type there may be evidence of human activity in the area in the drier times which is later covered by renewed peat growth. Since the preserving qualities of peat are excellent, organic material may survive in good condition.

BLANKET PEAT *on a hillside above Knockan Rock, north-west Scotland.*

Bloom
This is the name given to the metallic iron produced from the smelting process (q.v.). It is a solid, spongy mass of material which may still contain particles of slag and impurities, most of which will be driven off in preliminary forging.

Bog iron
A source of workable iron ore frequently found in areas with sub-arctic or arctic climatic conditions. It is not a rock but a deposit formed where iron-bearing surface waters, such as lakes, are in contact with organic material and iron oxides are precipitated. As the name suggests, it is common in bogs and in lake beds. If the deposition is continuous it can be a renewable resource. It can be worked like other iron, though it may be of lesser quality than rock ores.

Brachycephalic *see* CEPHALIC INDEX

Brass
An alloy of copper and zinc, the proportions ranging from 70–90% copper and 30–10% zinc. Perhaps due to difficulties in introducing the zinc ore calamine into the melt, brass appeared later in use than bronze and other copper alloys.

Breccia
The name given to a deposit of angular rock fragments detached from the parent cliff and consolidated in a calcitic matrix. Its occurrence denotes a previous cold phase in the climate, since the rock is detached through the agency of frost or alternating heat and cold. It is a typical deposit of caves, and is frequently found alternating with layers containing human occupation material.

Bristlecone pine
This tree, *Pinus aristata*, is the oldest living tree in the world. Its habitat is

parts of North America, where some living examples are over 4,000 years old. The combination of these and some well-preserved dead examples have allowed a dendrochronological (q.v.) key to be built up, which has led to changes in the assumptions underlying radiocarbon dating (q.v.), and to the provision of a calibration (q.v.) for radiocarbon dates going back some 7,000 years.

Bronze
An alloy of copper and tin in the proportions of approximately 90% copper and 10% tin. Much bronze had only trace elements (q.v.) apart from these two constituents, though the addition of lead, arsenic or antimony is known (*see* lead bronze; arsenical bronze; antimonial bronze). The addition of tin to copper makes casting easier and the edges of tools and weapons harder. A higher percentage of tin produces potin (q.v.) or speculum (q.v.).

Bulb of percussion
In flint-making, a flake or blade is struck off a core with a hammerstone. The point at which the hammerstone strikes is called the point of percussion, and on the flake struck off there is a rounded, slightly convex shape around this point called the bulb of percussion. On the core there is a corresponding concave bulb. The point and the bulb of percussion are rarely present if a flake has been struck off naturally, for example due to water causing a flint to strike another rock, or by frost fracture. Thus the presence of a bulb of percussion is a helpful guide towards the identification of a deliberately struck flint.

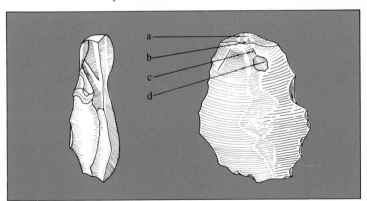

A flint, showing a. *striking platform;* b. *point of percussion;* c. BULB OF PERCUSSION; d. *bulbar scar.*

Bulbar scar
Term which describes the irregularly shaped scar to be found on the bulb of percussion (q.v.) of a struck flint flake which marks the place where a small piece of flint is dislodged during fracture.

Opposite *Living and dead* BRISTLECONE PINES *on a high slope of the White Mountains in California.*

Buried soil

An ancient land surface which has lain undisturbed since being covered by a still-standing monument or by naturally accumulating deposits like peat. Since it reflects the nature of the soil, at least at a very local level, at the time the monument was erected or the natural deposit laid down, its analysis for molluscan, faunal, pollen and insect remains should yield important information about the environmental conditions of the period.

Ref.: DIMBLEBY, G. W. and SPEIGHT, M. C. D. 'Buried soils', *Advancement of Science London* 26 (1969), 203–5.

Burnish

A form of pottery decoration in which the surface of the pot is polished, often using a spatula of wood or bone, while it is still in a leathery 'green' state, i.e. before firing. After firing the surface is extremely shiny. Often the whole outer surface of the pot is thus decorated, but in certain ceramic traditions there is 'pattern burnishing' where the outside and, in the case of open bowls, the inside, are decorated with burnished patterns in which some areas are left matt.

BURNISH *A black-burnished cooking pot from Redcliff, near Wareham, Dorset. 1st–2nd century* AD. *Height 18.5 cm.*

Calibration

In the context of radiocarbon dating (q.v.), this term refers to the adjustment of dates in radiocarbon years by means of the dendrochronological data so that a date in real, i.e. calendar, years is achieved. Uncalibrated dates, therefore, are raw dates in radiocarbon years, and this is the way that most dates from this technique are published.

Carination
A particular shape in vessels of metal or pottery. They are normally of bucket or jar shape, and have a sharply angled shoulder dividing the body of the vessel from the neck. Generally thought in the past to be a purely stylistic feature derived from metal prototypes, the carination may have had a practical function, for example for retaining dregs or such like from a liquid while pouring.

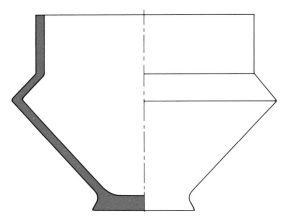

CARINATION *A sharply carinated pot from grave 057 of the Iron Age cemetery at Pernant, Aisne, France. Height 16cm. (*after *Lobjois 1969).*

Carrying capacity
The maximum population of a given species which can be supported by the food potentially available to it from the biological resources of an area. Studies of both human and animal groups in fact suggest that populations seldom reach such a theoretical maximum level, but adjust themselves to a size which allows a margin for fluctuations in the actual food production in the area.

Casting jet
When casting metal into a bivalve or composite mould (q.v.), the aperture through which the metal is poured into the mould becomes filled up with molten metal, and this plug of metal cools and hardens with the object. When the finished artefact is removed from the mould, the casting jet is still attached; in most cases it is knocked off and the scar polished down, the metal plug being melted down for re-use. In some cases, however, it may be left on, particularly on neckrings and bracelets, whether as pure decoration or as the mark of some social status is not known.

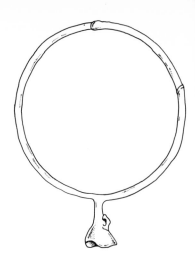

A neckring from a grave at Allendorf a. d. Lumda, Kr. Giessen, Germany, 6th century BC, *with* CASTING JET *retained as decoration. Diameter 15 cm. (*after *Schumacher 1972).*

Casting seam

When molten metal is poured into a bivalve or composite mould (q.v.), a small amount may seep between the surfaces of the two (or more) parts of the mould. The resulting visible seam when the object is removed from the mould is almost always filed and polished off, but occasionally unfinished objects are found with the seam still visible.

Catastrophe theory

A mathematical theory which demonstrates how, in a system comprising three or more variables, a small change in one variable can produce a sudden discontinuity in another. Its appeal to archaeologists lies in the fact that it shows how sudden changes can stem from comparatively small variations. Its application to archaeological problems presents many difficulties, but it has been used to explain the dramatic change in settlement patterns or the collapse of Maya and Mycenaean civilization by comparatively small changes in internal factors without the necessity of external influences such as invasions or natural disaster.

Central place theory

A theory concerning the spatial organization of sites offering goods or services to a surrounding region, first developed by the German geographer Walter Christaller in a study of modern towns in southern Germany. Central places are those towns or larger sites in a settlement system that act as centres for regional communities by providing economic, religious or administrative services. If it is assumed that the region is uniform in terrain and in the distribution of population, and that transport costs are equal in all directions, then the area served by any one centre in isolation would be circular. If it is further assumed that all centres in a region are of equal size and function, then in order to eliminate either gaps or overlapping, the pattern of circles should be transformed to one of equal interlocking hexagons with equidistant centres. Christaller's theory concentrated on centres of different order, since in a complex

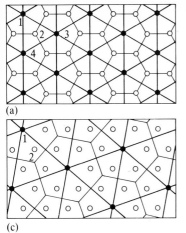

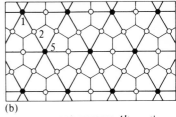

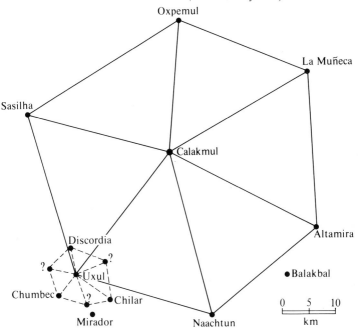

CENTRAL PLACE THEORY *Alternative principles of organization in the Christaller model:* a. *Market optimising K = 3.* b. *Traffic optimising K = 4.* c. *Administration optimising K = 7.* Below *An example of the application of central place theory to a real settlement pattern in the Maya lowlands, showing secondary centres grouped in a hexagon around central Calakmul, with the possibility of smaller sites grouped around Uxul* (after *Flannery 1976*).

system there will be some larger centres offering more specialized services to a wider area; there may indeed be many levels of such centres in a complex settlement hierarchy. The relationship between such centres of different orders could be organized in various ways, and Christaller distinguished three in particular. In a system based on marketing, each lower-order site will be located with equal access to three higher-order sites, and each higher-order site will serve itself and part of each of the six surrounding sites; this is termed the $\kappa = 3$ system, where κ is the number of sites served by a centre (in this case, itself plus one-third of each of the six lower-order sites). In a system based on transport, the lower-order sites will be located on main lines of communication at the mid-points between higher-order sites, each thus dependent on two such centres; this will give a $\kappa = 4$ system, each centre serving itself and one-half of the six surrounding sites. In a system based on administrative principles, the lower-order sites will be located wholly within the area of the higher-order site; this is a $\kappa = 7$ pattern (the centre plus the six dependent sites). Christaller's model has been modified by subsequent geographers, especially August Lösch; in his formulation, the settlements can form a nearly continuous sequence of centres rather than the distinct tiers of the hierarchy imposed by Christaller, so that sites of the same size need not serve the same function, and larger places need not perform all the functions of smaller centres.

The assumptions of uniformity of terrain, population and transport costs are in many cases obviously impractical, but the theory may suggest ways in which these factors have affected the settlement pattern. It has also been objected that a theory developed from a study of modern economic relationships in an industrialized society is not relevant to archaeological material, but the theory does fit many cases. The services offered may be administrative control or redistributive exchange rather than retail marketing, but the spatial pattern of sites is similar. The theory has been applied to the location and functioning of Roman towns, the emergence of centres in Mesoamerica and the centres of the medieval feudal system, for example.

Ref.: HODDER, I. and ORTON, C. *Spatial Analysis in Archaeology.* Cambridge, 1976, 60–4.

Cephalic index
The cephalic index is the definition of the relationship between the measurements of length and breadth of a human skull. The breadth of the skull is expressed as a percentage of the length: this produces an index which defines the skull as round-headed (brachycephalic), long-headed (dolichocephalic), or in-between. In the past, measurements based on incomplete skulls and without sufficiently accurate measuring devices have led those examining the anthropological data from archaeological sites to suggest that certain groups of people (e.g. 'Beaker' people) had predominantly one shape of head, but more recent work shows that varieties of cephalic indices may occur in a single population, even in the past before the present mixing of cultures.

Ceramic petrology
The study of the petrology of pottery, i.e. the examination and identifi-

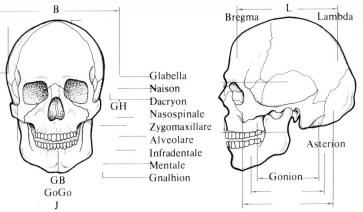

The points of the skull from which measurements are made to calculate CEPHALIC INDEX *(after Brothwell 1963).*

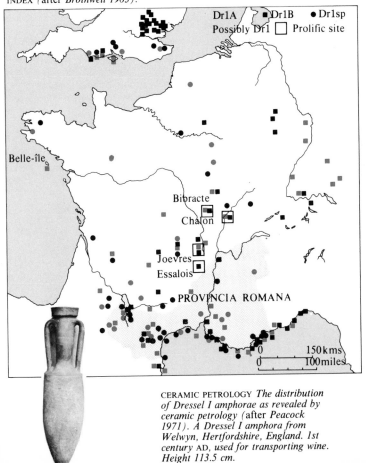

CERAMIC PETROLOGY *The distribution of Dressel I amphorae as revealed by ceramic petrology (after Peacock 1971). A Dressel I amphora from Welwyn, Hertfordshire, England. 1st century* AD, *used for transporting wine. Height 113.5 cm.*

cation of the minerals in the clay from which pottery is manufactured. The means by which the petrology is carried out are normally either heavy mineral analysis (q.v.) or petrological microscopy (q.v.), both of which require samples to be removed from the pot. Neutron activation analysis (q.v.) is also used. The aim of ceramic petrology is to locate the source of the clay from which the pot was made. If a particular clay can be identified as coming from a particular spot, then it is likely that the pots were made in that area. This has been shown by the analysis of pottery found far from its clay source; it is unlikely that the clay itself was transported, since the pots show traits in design and technique which reflect a single manufacturing area. Results of ceramic petrological studies have far-reaching consequences for the study of early economic systems. Not only has it been shown that pottery and its contents was transported over long distances in antiquity, but also that the specialized manufacture and marketing of pottery started much earlier than previously imagined, well back into the period of the first agriculturalists in Europe.

Ref.: PEACOCK, D. P. S. (ed.). *Pottery and Early Commerce.* London, 1977.

Champlevé
A technique of inlay working associated with the decoration of metals. The object to be decorated was provided with sunken areas, either in the original casting or cut out later, which were then filled with enamel frit (q.v.) and fused in an oven, or with polished stones or shells.

A silver-gilt brooch from Ash, Kent, England, late 6th century AD, showing the CHAMPLEVÉ inlay technique.

Chasing
A technique for the decoration of metalwork. Strictly chasing refers to line decoration applied to the face of repoussé (q.v.) work with a tracer (q.v.), but the term is frequently used more generally to describe any hammered or punched decoration on metal.

Chert
A coarse type of siliceous rock, a form of chalcedony, used for the manufacture of stone tools in areas where flint was not available. Flint, chert and other siliceous rocks like obsidian are very hard, and produce a razor-sharp edge when properly flaked into tools.

Chi-square test

A statistical test which measures the discrepancy between sets of observed values and those which would be expected, and assesses whether the departure from expectation is more than random chance would suggest. It can be used for many different archaeological observations, for instance to examine the existence of an association between settlement distribution and distinct ecological zones in a region, or between different fabrics and decorative styles in pottery production. From the observed data (e.g. the sizes of the various zones and the total number of sites in a region), the number expected in each zone on a random distribution can be calculated by proportion, and the discrepancy between expectation and observation measured. It is then possible to assess whether the observed data could have arisen by chance, or whether some other factor is affecting it.

Chiefdom

A form of social organization characterized by the existence of a chief who exercises central authority at the head of a social hierarchy in which an individual's status (q.v.) is determined by birth and nearness of relationship to the chief. The chief occupies a central role socially, politically and economically; chiefdoms generally practise redistribution (q.v.). This enables some development of craft specialization to take place, and chiefdoms are frequently marked by artistic or architectural achievements. The central authority enables considerable human effort to be mobilized and directed, often into the erection of large public works such as monuments or irrigation schemes. The most complex of chiefdoms may be hard to distinguish from states, but they lack the essential monopoly of force to back up their decisions.

Chromatography

So-named because the technique was originally used to separate coloured substances, this method of analysis involves the separation and subsequent identification of substances from a mixture by noting their different rate of movement along a liquid or solid column. It is particularly used for the identification of organic substances, and can be useful for the characterization of sources, as it has been for amber. There are several methods of chromatography, but particularly used in archaeology are paper and gas. In the former, a solution of the substance to be examined is placed at the end of a piece of filter paper; the end is then dipped into a solvent which moves the constituents of the sample along the paper by capillary action. Different substances reach different points on the filter paper and, by comparison with reference substances, can be identified. Gas chromatography is similar; the mixture is introduced into a column of material and is carried through by gases, the measurements of the gas emerging over time being made by a gas detector. The use of gas chromatography in the study of amber has shown that different sources produce different chromatograms.

Ref.: STOCK, R. and RICE, C. B. F. *Chromatographic Methods.* London, 1963, 2nd ed. 1967.

Chronometric dating

Techniques of dating which give the result in calendar years before the present, or B.P. Although the majority of these techniques produce results with a standard deviation (q.v.), they have a relationship to the calendar which relative dating (q.v.) techniques do not. Among the most useful chronometric dating techniques are radiocarbon dating (q.v.), potassium argon dating (q.v.), and thermoluminescence dating (q.v.), while dendrochronology (q.v.), with its linking of trees alive in the present to trees which died thousands of years ago, and no standard deviation, is the most accurate of all, though not universally applicable. The advent of chronometric dating in the last thirty years has revolutionized archaeology.

Cire perdue

A metalworking technique concerned with the casting process. The term (Fr.: lost wax) defines the following procedure. A model of the object required to be cast is made in wax, solid if the object is to be of solid metal, or built round a clay core if it is to be hollow. The wax model is covered with clay, and the whole is then heated to allow the wax to melt and run off; this leaves a space into which molten metal is poured. After it has cooled the outside clay is knocked off, the inner core, may be removed, and remaining is a metal version of the original wax model. Since the 'mould'

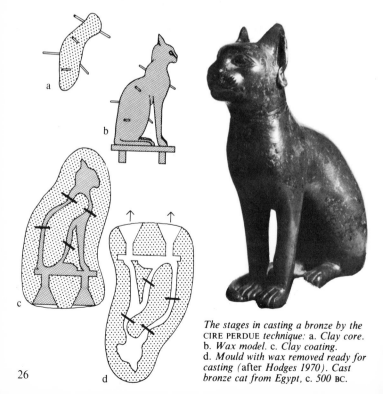

The stages in casting a bronze by the CIRE PERDUE *technique:* a. *Clay core.* b. *Wax model.* c. *Clay coating.* d. *Mould with wax removed ready for casting (*after Hodges 1970*). Cast bronze cat from Egypt, c. 500 BC.*

26

cannot be used again, each version of an object made using this technique is unique, and the process is more time consuming than making a complex mould and re-using it. However, more detail can be accomplished with the cire perdue process. The technique has been used from the early days of metalworking in all parts of the world, and for various metals—copper, bronze, silver and gold.

Cloisonné

This is a technique used for applying cells of enamel or other inlay to metal objects. The cells are created by soldering wire to the backing metal, each wire barrier dividing two cells of colour. The technique is somewhat similar to champlevé (q.v.), but it allows more intricacy of design.

A gold and silver brooch from Sarre, Kent, England, early 7th century AD, *showing the* CLOISONNÉ *inlay technique.*

Cluster analysis *see* NUMERICAL TAXONOMY

Coil-building

A method of making pottery in which a rope of clay, one long or several short, is coiled round on a flat base and continued on up to form the walls of a pot. The layers of clay are pressed together, and the inside and outside smoothed off to remove the lines between the coils, but frequently this is not done completely, and the coils may still be visible. Pottery often breaks along the coil lines.

Collagen content

Bone contains fats and protein or collagen. After death the fats disappear rapidly, but the collagen takes much longer to decay. Thus the collagen content of a bone yields information as to its relative date; this is measured by testing for the amount of nitrogen present (nitrogen test, q.v.).

Computer simulation

The exploration of how a cultural system behaves by the use of a computer to make repeated experiments of the effects of time and different conditions. In a study of hunter-gatherers, for instance, the effect of various changes in the natural environment on such factors as population, settlement pattern or subsistence could be monitored; or the growth of a settlement system could be studied under different conditions of popu-

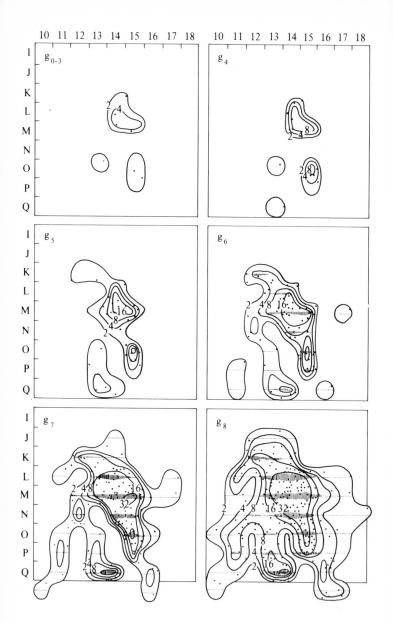

COMPUTER SIMULATION *A simulation of the process of diffusion produced by a computer (*after *Hägerstrand 1953).*

lation growth, economy and technological or environmental change. The relationships between the various elements in the cultural system must be specified, and then any variety of actual conditions can be simulated. The data used could be derived from real observations, and the simulation used to examine the effect of different assumptions; the results could then be compared to the real data to test their validity. Alternatively, randomly generated data could be used as the starting point for the study of general relationships.

Context

The spatial and chronological setting of an artefact or culture. The context of a find is its position on a site, its relationship through association with other artefacts, and its chronological position as revealed through stratigraphy. Certain features or artefacts may be normally associated with particular contexts, for example a pot type may be usually found in the context of a burial. If found out of context, it may suggest the previous presence of a burial, the robbery of a burial, or a place of manufacture of pots destined to accompany a burial.

Contingency table

A table which records the relationship between two classes of items, each entry counting the number of specific occurrences of the possible combinations. The classes compared in such a cross tabulation might be, for instance, sites in different ecological zones, artefacts in different contexts, or the coincidence of different decorative traits and fabric types in a pottery assemblage. Various statistics can be calculated from such a table, especially to test the significance of the observed correlations; the chi-square test (q.v.) is often used to do this.

Coprolite

Fossilized human or animal excreta; the study of these remains is called coprology. Coprolites only survive in exceptional circumstances, occasionally waterlogged but usually in arid cave deposits. They can be reconstituted by the addition of chemicals like trisodium phosphate, and can then be analysed for their plant and animal remains. This gives additional insight into what was being eaten on a site, since the evidence from pollen analysis (q.v.), or flotation (q.v.), only suggests what was being grown.

Ref.: CALLEN, E. O. 'Diet as revealed by coprolites', in *Science in Archaeology.* ed. D. Brothwell and E. Higgs. 2nd ed. London, 1969, 235–43.

Coprology

The study of coprolites (q.v.), which consists of the examination of fossil excreta, the extraction and identification of the constituents, and the analysis of the results in terms of diet.

Cordon

In ceramic technology a cordon is a strip of clay added around the outside of a pot for decoration or to help with handling. The cordon may be decorated in some way, for example with fingertip impressions. There may be more than one cordon on a pot. On a wheel-turned pot the cordons may be created by pushing the clay out in a narrow ring from inside, achieving a similar effect. In metalworking, a cordon is formed in much the same way as for a wheel-turned pot, that is, by the repoussé (q.v.) technique.

CORDON *A Bronze Age biconical urn from Barrow 68, Amesbury, Wiltshire, with applied cordons. Height 39 cm.*

Composite mould

A type of mould for manufacturing metal objects which can have three pieces or more. In its simplest form it may be a bivalve mould (q.v.) with the addition of a third part, a plug which will form a socket in the artefact when it is removed. More complex moulds than this can be used to cast more complex artefacts.

Coversand

A sediment of wind-blown sand which occurs mainly in coastal regions but also occasionally inland. It is formed by the carrying of sand grains from glacial outwash deposits or from the shore by gusts of wind which deposit the material as they die down. This may happen repeatedly, so that the material may eventually end up several kilometres from its source. In areas where it occurs, it may completely obliterate evidence of occupation prior to the formation of the deposit, and it is therefore necessary to examine below what is apparently natural sand for pre-sand levels.

Crop-mark *see* AERIAL PHOTOGRAPHY

Cross-dating

A relative dating technique (q.v.) which can theoretically be a chronometric dating technique (q.v.) if the material used for the technique is narrowly restricted in time. The basis of cross-dating is the occurrence of finds in association (q.v.). The assumption is that a particular type of artefact, for example a sword type, when found in an undated context will bear a similar date to one found in a dated context, thus enabling the whole of the undated context to be given a chronological value. Many of the chronologies constructed before the advent of chronometric dating techniques were based on cross-dating, though the method was sometimes used with little precision: absolute dates were available from historical chronologies recorded in the Near East, and attempts were made to extrapolate from these, by several intermediate steps, to areas well beyond the range of Near Eastern artefacts. Similarities of form in artefacts were allowed as much weight as actual imports. New dating techniques such as radiocarbon (q.v.) showed some of the links established by cross-dating to be invalid, so that aspects of the method have become somewhat discredited. However, its use is still clearly helpful where recognizable products of dateable manufacture are found in undated contexts with no possibility of using a chronometric dating technique.

Culture

A word with several different uses and meanings. In a general sense it applies to the whole way of life of man as a species, and in a more specific usage to the way of life of a particular social group, such as Eskimo culture. In both these usages it has been defined in many different ways. Many archaeologists have regarded culture as an inherited set of ideas or norms which prescribe how things shall be made or done within the community; the archaeologist's task is then to reconstruct these ideas from the cultural products of the society. An alternative view of culture sees it as the set of methods, excluding those which are directly controlled by genetics, by which a group or individual adjusts itself to its human and natural environment. In this evolutionary view, the emphasis is on the adaptation, with culture as the humanly controlled counterpart of the biological evolution of man. The word culture has also been used in a very different sense, to describe a collection of archaeologically observable data; it is defined as the regularly occurring assemblage of associated artefacts and practices, such as pottery, house-types, metalwork and burial rites, and regarded in this sense as the physical expression of a particular social group. This usage is especially associated with Gordon Childe, who popularized this concept as a means of analysing prehistoric material.

Cyclic agriculture

This term defines a hypothetical process suggested as having been in existence among early agriculturalists. Before the use of fertilisers and other efficient farming methods, cultivated land around a settlement loses its fertility in time and eventually becomes unproductive unless it is allowed to lie fallow for a while. It is suggested that an early farming site might have been exploited for a decade, and then left while the inhabitants founded a new settlement not too far away, farming that too for a decade before moving on again. If ten sites were settled in this way, forming a rough circle, in the eleventh decade the original site could be resettled, the land having regained its fertility naturally after a century of lying fallow. There is no proof of this process occurring in antiquity, though its use is suspected in certain areas, for example in Eastern Europe.

Damascening

Although related to pattern-welding (q.v.), this technique used in the manufacture of sword blades probably developed independently. First a high-carbon steel was produced by firing wrought iron and wood together in a sealed crucible; the resulting steel, or wootz, consists of light cementations in a darker matrix, and this, together with a series of complicated forging techniques at relatively low temperatures produced the delicate 'watered silk' pattern with the alternating high- and low-carbon areas. Damascene steel was very strong and highly elastic.

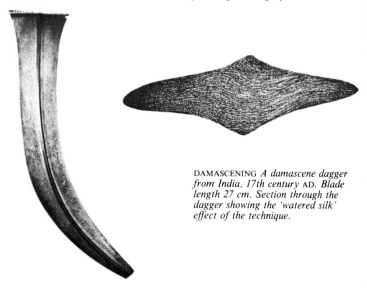

DAMASCENING *A damascene dagger from India, 17th century* AD. *Blade length 27 cm. Section through the dagger showing the 'watered silk' effect of the technique.*

Ref.: MARYON, H. 'Pattern-welding and damascening of sword blades', *Studies in Conservation* 5 (1960), 52–60.

Datum point

The point on an archaeological site from which all measurements of level and contour are taken. It can be chosen at random, at a place from which all or most of the site can be seen, and should be tied in to the national height scale by reference to the nearest survey point. Depths of features, of objects found in features, or simply contours, are levelled (level, q.v.) in with reference to the datum point, and are usually recorded as being a certain height 'below Local Datum'. Should variations in contour or the extent of the site prove too great for a single datum point, another can be used as long as it is levelled in with reference to the first.

Daub

Clay which is plastered onto a structure of timber or wattle as a finish to the surface. It also acts as a draught excluder, and is normally added to both faces of a wall. The material usually survives only when baked or fire-hardened, as would be the case if a structure burned down. It can usually be recognized by the impressions of the wattle to be found on its inner face.

A piece of DAUB *with wattle impressions from a Saxon site at Swindon Hill, Wiltshire, England.*

Deep sea cores

A technique used in the analysis of data from oceanic sediments. The material retrieved by the core yields information on temperature changes in the ocean through time. These changes, suggestive of climatic variation, help to chart the progress of glaciation and, since they can be dated, the technique can assist in the establishment of a chronology for Palaeolithic sequences. The cores, some 5cm. in diameter and up to 25m. deep, are extracted from the ocean floor. The sediments they contain have a high percentage of calcium carbonate content made up of the shells of small marine organisms like *Foraminifera*. Since these organisms have different temperature preferences depending on species, the relative abundance of the various species changes as the temperature alters. Through the identification of the species, and by the use of oxygen isotope analysis (q.v.), a picture can be built up of variations in temperature over the millennia. Since various forms of dating (radiocarbon dating, q.v.; ionium dating, protactinium/ionium dating) can be used on the carbonate in the shells, in theory absolute dates can be given to the different levels in the core. Thus dates emerge for glaciations and interglacial periods, which can assist in the age determination of archaeological material found in association with these glacial phases. Problems with the technique are centred on the difficulty of correlating oceanic temperature changes with continental glacial and interglacial phases.

Ref.: SHACKLETON, N. J. and TURMER, C. 'Correlation of marine and terrestrial Pleistocene successions', *Nature* 216 (1967), 1079–82.

Dendrochronology

A chronometric (q.v.) dating technique which has the potential to be the most accurate of all these techniques, back to several thousand years BC in some areas. It is based on the principle that trees add a growth ring for each year of their lives, and that variations in climatic conditions will affect the width of these rings on suitable trees. In a very dry year growth will be restricted, and the ring narrow, while a wet and humid year will produce luxuriant growth and a thick ring. By comparing a complete series of rings from a tree of known date (for example, one still alive) with a series from an earlier, dead tree overlapping in age, ring patterns from the central layers of the recent tree and the outer of the old may show a correlation which allows the dating, in calendar years, of the older tree. The central rings of this older tree may then be compared with the outer rings of a yet older tree, and so on until the dates reach back into prehistory. This is the theory; in practice, the technique is not so simple for various reasons. First, climatic variation and suitable trees (sensitive trees react to climatic changes, complacent trees do not) may not be present to produce any significant and recognizable pattern of variation in the rings. Secondly, there may be gaps in the sequences of available timber, so that the chronology 'floats', or is not tied in to a calendrical date: it can only be used for relative dating in the area in which it is relevant. Then, as the climatic variations need only to be local to affect the rings, a dendrochronological sequence valid for one area may bear little resemblance to another constructed for a nearby area, so that many local chronologies have to be built up. Finally, the tree-ring key can only go back a certain distance into the past, since the availability of sufficient amounts of timber to construct a sequence obviously decreases. Only in a few areas of the world are there species of trees so long-lived that long chronologies can be built up (bristlecone pine, q.v.).

Despite these problems, dendrochronology is of immense importance for archaeology, not least for its contribution to the refining of radiocarbon dating (q.v.). Since timber can be dated by radiocarbon, dates may be obtained from dendrochronologically dated trees. It has been shown that the radiocarbon dates diverge increasingly from calendrical dates provided by tree-rings the further back into prehistory they go, the radiocarbon dates being younger than the tree-ring dates. This has allowed the questioning of one of the underlying assumptions of radiocarbon dating, the constancy of the concentration of C14 in the atmosphere. Fluctuations in this concentration have now been shown back as far as

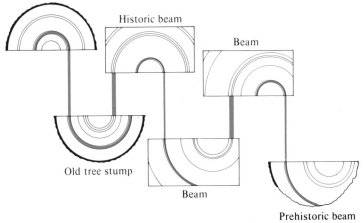

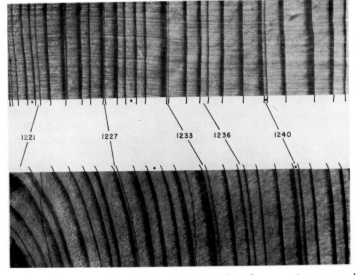

DENDROCHRONOLOGY Above *How a dendrochronological sequence is constructed (after Fagan 1972).* Below *Chronological links between two sensitive trees from Betatakin, Arizona, USA, demonstrating the technique of cross-dating by matching the rings.*

dendrochronological sequences go (to *c.* 7000 BC), and thus one dating technique is serving the further research on another.

Ref.: BANNISTER, B. 'Dendrochronology', in *Science in Archaeology,* ed. D. Brothwell and E. Higgs. 2nd ed. London, 1969, 191–205.

Dendrogram

A diagram in the form of a schematized tree with many branching lines at one end and uniting into a single trunk at the other. It is used particularly to show the clustering of similar items into groups; at one extreme each individual forms a separate group, but as the level of similarity within a group diminishes so the group gets larger, until all items can be classed into one group.

Dentition

The general characteristic arrangement of teeth in animal species. The study of dentition is an important part of the discipline of archaeozoology (q.v.), since it can not only be a major factor in the identification of animal remains, but can also be used to determine age in both man and animal, either from the state of eruption and replacement of milk teeth or to a certain extent from the amount of wear.

Diatom

This is a unicellular alga which inhabits watery deposits. Its cell wall is of silica. Because of their enhanced chances of survival due to the silica as

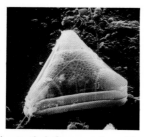

An electron-scanning micrograph of a DIATOM, Biddulphia alternans, *greatly enlarged.*

well as to their frequent deposition in anaerobic (q.v.) conditions, they can be located in archaeological as well as geological deposits. The different species are generally associated with specific habitats, and their analysis can therefore yield information on the changing environment, particularly at coastal sites.

Differential fluxgate gradiometer

An instrument used in magnetic surveying (q.v.) for detecting changes in the intensity of the magnetic field. This instrument has the advantage over a proton magnetometer (q.v.) of speed of operation, since readings can be obtained continually as opposed to individual spot measurements; the complex electronics, however, make it an expensive alternative to the proton gradiometer (q.v.). Two detectors containing mu-metal strips wound round with primary and secondary coils are mounted at either end of a staff which is carried vertically; an initial pure sine-wave voltage is applied, and the difference in intensities observed between the two detectors corresponds to disturbance in the magnetic field caused by baked clay or buried features. These differences are displayed on a meter on the instrument.

A DIFFERENTIAL FLUXGATE GRADIOMETER *in use in the field, Northamptonshire, England.*

Ref.: ALLDRED, J. C. 'A fluxgate gradiometer for archaeological surveying', *Archaeometry* 7 (1964), 14–19.

Diffusion

A definition of the spread of ideas, traits or peoples from one area to another. The movement of ideas and artefacts is not held necessarily to imply the movement of people, since trade and the adoption of new ideas from neighbouring cultures are reasonable explanations of diffusion. The diffusion of new ideas can come, however, from the peaceful or warlike expansion of a population into new territory. The theory of diffusion was used in the past to explain the beginning of most new ideas: it was assumed that technological skills such as metalworking, or the building of large monumental structures, could only have begun in one place, whence they diffused to other areas. It is now clear, through the advent of new dating techniques, that independent invention (q.v.) was certainly possible and probable for many new ideas. As a reaction against the explanation of all progress as a result of diffusion, the theory has been rejected out of hand by some archaeologists, though it is clear that some interaction between people, and therefore some exchange and diffusion of ideas, must have been happening continually throughout prehistory and history.

Direct percussion

This is a technique for the working of flint where the parent material is struck directly with another stone, the hammerstone, or a piece of wood, in order to dislodge a flake. The method is less precise in its results than indirect percussion (q.v.).

Directional trade *see* EXCHANGE

Distal

The part of a long bone (leg or arm) which is furthest from the body. The opposite end is the proximal.

Distance-decay function

A mathematical expression of the rate at which interaction declines as the distance from the source increases. Such a function, which is a specific example of linear regression analysis (q.v.), can be used to describe the relationship between the amount of a given commodity found at any point and the place from which it was exported. The patterns produced and the mathematical expressions used to describe them can help to distinguish different forms of exchange (q.v.). In general, distance-decay varies with the value of the object traded, with the richer items spreading further afield.

DISTANCE DECAY *An obsidian projectile point from the island of Melos, Cyclades.* Below *The map shows obsidian sources for the Near East and sites where the material was used (*after *Renfrew* et al *1968). Opposite *The diagram shows the fall-off in percentages of obsidian in the stone industries at various sites as distance from the source increases (*after *Renfrew* et al *1968).*

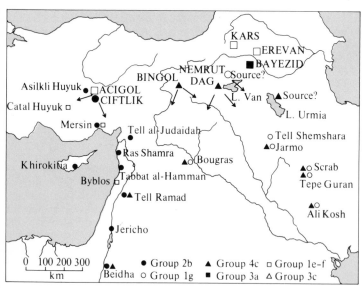

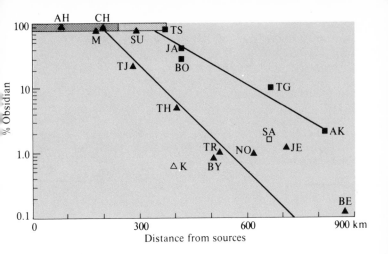

Distribution

A definition of the spatial location of artefacts, structures or settlement types in a landscape. Analysis of the distribution of a particular artefact type may lead to conclusions about the nature of the industry or culture which produced or used it. The distribution of objects is studied by the plotting of the find-places of the material in question on a distribution map: the relationship of the dots to the natural environment may reveal something about communication networks or the economic subsystem, while clustering of dots may suggest different cultural or technological entities. The overlaying of one trait on another may suggest association or sequence, while mutually exclusive distributions can imply contemporaneity. The drawback to this visual representation of distribution is the tendency to accept the information suggested by the distribution patterns (for example, clustering of finds suggesting central places) without thinking of the processes by which finds were deposited and the real reason for their eventual distribution. Gaps in distributions may reflect gaps in archaeological research rather than real gaps in distribution.

Dolichocephalic *see* CEPHALIC INDEX

Domestication

The controlling of natural fauna by early agriculturalists through selection and breeding so that animals might produce more of what man needed than their wild forebears. The definition includes the taming of cats and dogs as house pets, as well as the care and control of cattle, sheep, goat, pig, horse, llama, camel and guinea pig. Selective breeding for produce such as milk and meat, hides and wool, went alongside the training of animals for draught and carrying. This selection by man resulted in osteological changes in the animals, so that in general domesticated animals can be distinguished by their remains from their wild ancestors. However, the identification of domesticated animal bones from very early farming sites presents problems, since the selection procedure had only just begun (archaeozoology, q.v.).

Ref.: ZEUNER, F. E. *A History of Domesticated Animals.* London, 1963.

Down-the-line exchange *see* EXCHANGE

Ecofact
This is a useful term for defining floral and faunal material associated with archaeological sites. Seeds, pollen, animal bone, insects, fish bones and molluscs are all ecofacts.

Ecosystem
The total living community of a single environment—the flora, fauna, insects, and man himself—and the interactions of the constituent parts as well as their relationship with the non-organic environment.

Einkorn
One of the species of wheat which were first domesticated by early farmers (palaeoethnobotany, q.v.). It is a hulled grain (i.e. the glume remains on the grain after threshing), and has been found in its wild form, *Triticum boeoticum.* and its cultivated form, *Triticum monococcum.* from farming sites of the eighth and seventh millennia BC. Like the other cereals, it could be used for bread-making or for porridge.

Electromagnetic surveying
A technique for the location of archaeological features which uses the pulsed induction meter (q.v.) or the soil conductivity meter (q.v.). Though these instruments are theoretically able to locate features, as well as metal objects for which they are extremely suitable, in practice they only work at a very shallow level, and no electromagnetic instrument is as accurate as the resistivity (q.v.) meter or one of the magnetometers (proton gradiometer, q.v.; proton magnetometer, q.v.).

Electron probe microanalyser
This is a physical method of chemical analysis which can determine the constituent elements in metal, stone, glass and pottery though, like X-ray fluorescence spectrometry (q.v.), to which technique it is closely allied, the analysis is only of a thin surface layer of the sample. The technique is slightly destructive, requiring the removal of a small sample from the artefact. Instead of X-rays, as in X-ray fluorescence, an electron beam is used to excite the atomic electrons; the result, the emission of secondary X-rays with characteristic wavelengths for the elements concerned, is similar in the two techniques. The beam can be focussed on to a very small area of the specimen, and can be moved around to sample different points: thus the method is particularly useful for the study of surface enrichment in metals, and of pigments. Though the procedure for preparing specimens is more complex than that for X-ray fluorescence spectrometry, the

calculations of concentrations of elements are more straightforward, while the range of elements which can be analysed is comparable.

Ref.: HORNBLOWER, A. P. 'Archaeological applications of the electron probe microanalyser', *Archaeometry* 5 (1962), 108–12.

Electrum
A natural alloy of gold and silver from which precious artefacts were made. The process of extracting the silver from the gold is complex, and may not have been accomplished in the early stages of metalworking. A deliberate alloying of silver with gold, producing an electrum with often as much as 45% silver, was certainly carried out before the turn of the era.

Elm decline
A term defining a phase in the history of vegetation in Europe recognized through pollen analysis (q.v.), dated by radiocarbon (q.v.), but still a

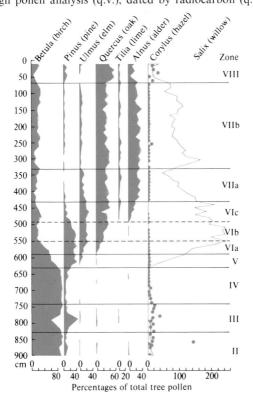

ELM DECLINE *A pollen diagram of Hockham Mere, Norfolk, showing the decline in elm pollen at the 340 cm. level (*after Godwin 1975*).*

41

subject of controversy regarding its significance. The phenomenon was noticed as a sudden and marked decline in elm pollen in relation to other tree pollens at around 3,000 bc in radiocarbon years (uncalibrated). In some areas it was accompanied by a drop in frost-sensitive species such as ivy and mistletoe, while in many others it coincided with the appearance of plants associated with human settlements like plantain and nettles. Some scholars considered a change in some climatic factor the most likely reason, but the majority now believe that there was a causal relationship between the elm decline and man's farming activities, possibly explained by the use of elm leaves as fodder for cattle and sheep during the time when land was being cleared for pasture.

Emmer
A wheat species cultivated by early farmers (palaeoethnobotany, q.v.); it is a hulled species (i.e. threshing does not remove the glumes from the grain). It is found in archaeological contexts in both its wild *(Triticum dicoccoides)* and its cultivated *(Triticum dicoccum)* form from the eighth millennium onwards.

Environmental archaeology
The study of the environment in archaeological contexts. It includes not only the study of past flora (pollen analysis, q.v.; palaeobotany, q.v.; palaeoethnobotany, q.v.; archaeobotany, q.v.) and fauna (archaeo-zoology, q.v.), but also that of insects (insect analysis, q.v.), fish (fish bone analysis, q.v.) and snail shells (molluscan analysis, q.v.). All are studied in an attempt to recover the total environment of a past society and to understand man's impact on, and changes to, that environment.

Ref.: EVANS, J. G. *An Introduction to Environmental Archaeology.* London, 1978.

Epiphyses
The articular ends of long bones or vertebrae which in an adult are fused with the shaft or main part of the bone, but which are separate bony masses in the early years of life. For both human and animal bones therefore, the state of fusion of the epiphyses can be used to determine the age of the skeleton if it is under 20 years old (human) or 3–4 years (domestic animals; *see* archaeozoology).

Ethnoarchaeology
A relatively new branch of the discipline of archaeology followed particularly in America. It seeks to compare the patterns recognized in the material culture from archaeological contexts with patterns yielded through the study of living societies. The ethnoarchaeologist is particularly concerned with the manufacture, distribution and use of artefacts, the remains of various processes that might be expected to survive, and the interpretation of archaeological material in the light of the ethnographic information. Less materially oriented questions such as technological development, subsistence strategies and social evolution are also com-

pared in archaeology and ethnology under the general heading of ethnographic analogy.

Ref.: STILES, D., 'Ethn'oarchaeology; a discussion of methods and applications', *Man* 12 (1977). 87–103.

Eustasy

This term defines the changing of the sea-level on a global basis, usually as the result of a major event such as the end of a glaciation. In such a case a eustatic rise due to the melting of the glaciers can be expected in a post-glacial period. These sea-level movements can be independent of any change in the height of the land, but isostasy (q.v.) can happen contemporaneously as a result of the same phenomenon.

Excavation

The main tool of the archaeologist, since without excavation he would recover only a fragment of the information available to him about man's past. The excavation of a site, however, whether on a small or massive scale, involves the destruction of the primary evidence, which can never be recovered nor repeated since no two sites are identical. Excavation should therefore never be undertaken lightly or without an understanding of the obligations of the excavator to the evidence he destroys. There are many processes involved in excavation, and many decisions to be taken. The first is whether to excavate a site at all, a question of particular interest when sites are being rapidly destroyed by the intensification of farming methods, the building of new roads, and the expansion of towns. Assuming that a policy of when to excavate what has been decided, and a particular site is to be excavated, the next problem is the nature and scale of the undertaking. If time and/or money is short, sampling (q.v.) of the site may be all that is possible. If a large-scale excavation is to be undertaken, the approach will probably be one of area excavation (q.v.), though in certain contexts the grid method (q.v.) may still be suitable. Removal of the topsoil will either be carried out by hand or machine, depending on its nature: if only a few centimetres of soil lie above the rock, or the ground is unploughed, then important information may come from the topsoil, and it should be hand-dug. If the topsoil has been deep-ploughed, then the removal of the top layer by machine will probably do little damage to the overall picture of the site, and will be much quicker. After an initial plan has been made of all visible features before excavation, digging proceeds according to the dictates of the site: sections (q.v.) may be taken across complicated areas of feature intersection, or across individual features, while the removal of coherent layers or levels of material will naturally follow where the stratigraphy is clear. A permanent record of the whole process should be kept: plans will be drawn at every stage where something new appears, drawings will be made of all sections cut, whether understood or not, and all finds will be recorded as coming from identifiable separate features or will be planned in in three dimensions so that their position in the site can be reconstructed later. A

EXCAVATION **Above** *Excavating by the grid method at the eastern entrance of Maiden Castle, Dorset, England.*
Below *Excavating a large area at Portway, Andover, Hampshire, England, where an area of 3½ acres was opened at one time.*

photographic record should also be kept, since photographs can nicely complement drawn material, and be used to record stages in the excavation of certain features which do not merit new plans. The use of levelling equipment (level, q.v.) allows the accurate measurement of depths, while the original marking of a site grid makes planning by triangulation (q.v.), offsets (q.v.), or grid a very simple procedure. After the excavation, the analysis of the stratigraphy and the extraction of the finds, the areas excavated may be filled in, though in some cases the excavation might be left permanently open as an exhibit. The excavation is only the first part of the process, since a site may as well not have been excavated until it has been published. Publication often takes longer than the original excavation, particularly where specialist reports (such as archaeobotany, archaeozoology, ceramic petrology) are awaited.

*Ref.:*BARKER, P. *Techniques of Archaeological Excavation.* London, 1977.

Exchange

Generally the transfer of goods between people. The term 'trade' may be used to mean the same, but it has more specific overtones of the formalized economic relationships of modern societies. Three different forms of the social organization of exchange are usually distinguished: reciprocity, redistribution, and market exchange; the term exchange is sometimes restricted specifically to the last of these three. The spatial patterns of traded items can reveal the mode of exchange. In 'down-the-line' exchange, for instance, where a commodity is passed successively from one group to another even further away from its source, the pattern will show a distinct decline in the quantity of the item as distance from the source increases; the higher the value of the item, the further it will reach. In 'directional exchange', where a commodity is traded directly from its source to a distant point without any intermediate exchange, the pattern of decreasing quantities with increasing distance will be distorted with a local concentration. (*See also* RECIPROCITY; REDISTRIBUTION).

Experimental archaeology

A term used to describe attempts at the reconstruction of past processes, the testing of hypotheses about the way in which man dealt with the problems of subsistence and technology. The term is normally used only for those experiments which deal with material culture, such as industry, the building of structures, mining and crop processing. The more theoretical aspects, such as ideas about the development and organization of society, are generally thought of as part of processual archaeology (q.v.) rather than experimental. There have been experiments in the study of archaeology since the nineteenth century, but there has been a dramatic increase in the last two decades. They range from reconstructions of metalworking, pottery manufacture and stoneworking to the planting,

EXPERIMENTAL ARCHAEOLOGY *An Iron Age house reconstucted as an experiment at Butser Hill, Hampshire, England.*

Ploughing with yoked oxen at the experimental Iron Age farm, Butser Hill, Hampshire, England.

Charred wood

Collapsed turf roof

Trench

Hearth

0 1 2 3 4 5

metres

Top *Reconstruction of an Iron Age house at Roskilde, Denmark (after Hansen 1966).* Bottom *Plan of the remains of the house as excavated after its experimental destruction by fire.*

harvesting and storage of food. There have been reconstructions, based on excavated ground plans, of various types of structure, and some of these have then been deliberately burned, or left to decay, so that an idea can be gained of what the archaeologist might expect to find later. Boats have been built and sailed, food has been cooked in earth ovens and eaten, stone monuments have been laboriously erected, and trumpets and stringed instruments have been made and played. The results of these processes which indicate what might be left for the archaeologist to find are among the most useful aspects of this work. In no case can an experiment be said to prove that a certain procedure was the one followed in antiquity, but it can point to possibilities, and on these grounds experimental archaeology has a valid role to play in attempts to reconstruct past societies.

Ref.: COLES, J. *Archaeology by Experiment.* London, 1973.

Extensive excavation *see* AREA EXCAVATION

Facies
A group of elements in an industry (q.v.) or culture (q.v.) which appears to be a sub-group, or a different aspect of, a main cultural tradition. A major division of a cultural sequence, such as the Mousterian 'culture' of the European Palaeolithic, is often described as having different facies (for example, the Quina Mousterian, or the Mousterian of Acheulian tradition), though these may reflect different industries or cultures. The term is confusing, since it is imprecise and yet appears to 'explain'; it is used less frequently now than earlier.

Faience
This term is applied to two types of material; it therefore means two different things depending on the context. In the field of medieval pottery, it describes a form of majolica ware characteristic of Faenza in Italy. The name is otherwise applied to a material made of powdered quartz and alkali which were mixed to a paste with water and then fired to a point where a vitreous mass, a cross between clay and glass, was produced. Coloured with copper salts to produce a blue-green finish, it was used especially for beads and figurines in the Near East and particularly in the second millennium BC.

False colour infra-red photography
A technique used in aerial photography that was developed outside archaeology but is now much employed, especially in the Americas. The infra-red film reacts to the varying water absorption qualities of different features, and thus changes in vegetation, the occurrence of buried features filled with disturbed soil, the presence of otherwise invisible roadways may be detected. The false colour refers to the accentuation of specific features in red, pink, yellow, blue, etc., which bear no relationship to natural colour but which emphasize the contrasts. (*See* the cover.)

Feature
In excavation, this term defines any constituent of an archaeological site which is not classed as a find or a small find (q.v.). Ditches, gullies, pits, wells, walls, ovens, hearths, graves, postholes, sleeper-beam trenches, stakeholes and palisade trenches, are all features. The term is even more useful for constituents which cannot be defined as clearly as these— amorphous blobs or stains to which no reasonable classification can be applied.

Filigree
A special form of decorative gold or silver work. It consists of creating a pattern out of, for example, gold wire which is soldered together and to the main body of the piece. The wire can be plain or decorative in section; for goldwork, the solder was normally a gold-copper alloy (82% gold, 18% copper), which had a lower melting point than pure gold.

Fishbone analysis
The remains of fish on archaeological sites are in the form of bones, otoliths (q.v.) and scales. The latter only survive occasionally in anaerobic (q.v.) conditions, while otoliths have not, to date, been frequently recorded. Fishbones often survive in archaeological deposits, but until recently have often not been located since many are so small that they may only appear in sieving. Since the increased interest in environmental archaeology (q.v.) in general, and the sieving of samples from archaeological deposits for a variety of remains (faunal, insect, seed, molluscan), much more evidence has been revealed. Under normal circumstances vertebrae are recoverable, as well as a lot of smaller bones when careful techniques are employed. Identification of species through comparison with modern fishbones is becoming easier as larger collections of comparative material are built up. When a species has been identified it can lead to evidence for the hydrological conditions around the site; also, the occurrence of the remains of marine species on an inland site has implications for the movement of groups or a trade in fish. A combination of species identification and ageing of fish through study of the otoliths (q.v.) can lead to assumptions about the seasonal occupation of certain settlement sites and the subsistence economy of the associated groups.

Ref.: CASTEEL, R. W. *Fish Remains in Archaeology and Palaeo-Environmental Studies.* London, 1976.

Fission track dating
A chronometric dating technique which may be useful for dating volcanic substances such as obsidian, man-made glass, and the mineral inclusions in pottery. The basis for this technique is that a uranium isotope, U 238, as well as decaying to a stable lead isotope, also undergoes spontaneous fission. One in every two million atoms decays in this way. Fission is accompanied by an energy release which sends the resulting two nuclei

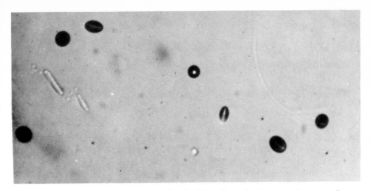

FISSION TRACK DATING *Examples of etched fossil tracks in natural materials.*

into the surrounding material, the tracks causing damage to the crystal lattice. These tracks can be counted under an optical microscope after the polished surface of the sample has been etched with acid. The concentration of uranium can be determined by the induced fission of U 235 by neutron irradiation of the sample. Since the ratio of U 235 to U 238 is known, and is constant, a comparison of the number of tracks from natural fission and the number from induced fission will give the age of the sample. Though the method has been limited in its archaeological use so far, it has already proved a useful check method for potassium-argon dating (q.v.) for volcanic deposits at Olduvai Gorge, Tanzania, and obsidian and some man-made glasses have also been dated. A further use of the method is based on the fact that fission tracks disappear if the substance is heated above 500° or so: thus a date achieved for clay (like a hearth), pottery or obsidian that had been burnt gives the date of burning or firing, since previous fission tracks would have disappeared.

Ref.: FLEISCHER, R. L., PRICE, P. B. and WALKER, R. M. 'Nuclear tracks in solids', *Scientific American* 220 (1969), 30–39.

Floating chronology

A segment of chronometrically (q.v.) dated time which is not yet tied in to calendar years. The most common floating chronologies occur in dendrochronology (q.v.) where climate affects the growth of rings and therefore sequences are local. These local sequences cannot always be tied in to the master sequences established in certain areas from the present day back into prehistory, and therefore the local sequences will 'float' until some link with a known historical date is found. Similarly, in magnetic dating (q.v.) many of the sequences will float until some independently dated sites can be entered on the curve.

Flot

A term relatively recently coined from the technique of flotation (q.v.); it is used to describe the material which floats on water or other relevant media during the flotation process. It therefore includes plant remains such as seeds and charcoal, insect remains such as the wing-cases of beetles, and land snail-shells, as well as miscellaneous intrusive modern material like plant roots which must be sorted from the sample before analysis.

Flotation

An important technique developed to assist in the recovery of plant, insect and molluscan remains from archaeological deposits (palaeoethno-botany, archaeobotany, insect analysis, molluscan analysis, q.v.). The technique works on the principle that organic material such as carbonised seeds, snail-shells and beetle wing-cases have a lower specific gravity than inorganic materials such as soil and stone, and will thus float on the top of a suitable liquid medium while the rest will sink. Water is commonly used for flotation, though there are disadvantages since it has a fairly low specific gravity and heavier material such as fruit stones will sink. Other media have been used, such as carbontetrachloride solution or zinc chloride solution, but these also have certain disadvantages. Depending on the scale of excavation and the size of the deposits, as well as the sampling strategy, flotation may be carried out by hand or by machine. Flotation of samples by hand is called wet sieving (q.v.). Samples of material are slowly poured into water, any lumps are broken up, and the flot (q.v.) is drawn off with a sieve. The method is more controlled than flotation by machine, and the recovery rate is doubtless better. However, for large-scale excavations this method is usually too time consuming, as well as needing a lot of manpower, and machines are used instead. These are of varying types and are normally built out of discarded materials, hence they vary in design. Operating principles also vary: samples are poured into a large container of water, or water and paraffin, which is agitated by air injection or by currents of inflowing water. The addition of a floculating agent increases surface tension, though not all machines are 'froth flotation' machines. The flot is carried off the surface through a mesh, or series of meshes to allow preliminary sorting. Samples thus retrieved are sent away for specialist identification and analysis by an archaeobotanist.

A simple FLOTATION *machine for the recovery of organic material from archaeological deposits: the 'Ankara' machine (after* **Renfrew** *et al* **n.d.**).

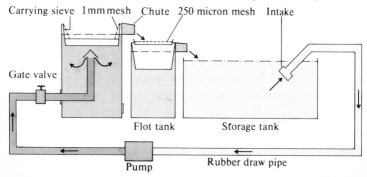

Carrying sieve   1mm mesh   Chute   250 micron mesh   Intake

Gate valve

Flot tank   Storage tank

Pump   Rubber draw pipe

Fluorine test

A technique for establishing the relative date of bones. It is based on the fact that the inorganic phosphatic mineral hydroxyapatite, contained in bone, is altered after burial into fluorapatite as a result of fluorine from percolating ground waters coming into contact with the bone. The change is irreversible, and increases with time, so that chemical analysis can demonstrate the content of fluoride in the bone and therefore the length of time that it has been buried. Local conditions such as the amount of groundwater and the type of burial medium affect the rate of fluorine accumulation, and therefore the technique produces relative rather than absolute chronological values. Contemporaneity or non-contemporaneity of bones in the same deposit can be demonstrated, especially when the technique is allied with nitrogen tests (q.v.) and uranium tests (q.v.).

Ref.: OAKLEY, K. P. 'Analytical methods of dating bones', in *Science in Archaeology*, ed. D. Brothwell and E. Higgs, 2nd ed. London, 1969, 35–45.

Fluxgate gradiometer *see* DIFFERENTIAL FLUXGATE GRADIOMETER

Forging

The main process for the working of iron and steel after smelting (q.v.). Though copper and other metals can be worked cold with occasional annealing (q.v.), this is not a suitable procedure for iron and steel. Forging involves the heating of the bloom (q.v.) to red heat, and hammering; in the first instance this would be carried out on a flat anvil with a hammer, and the main aim would be to remove impurities and the remains of slag. The resulting bars of iron could then be thinned down and hammered into shape again, continuously heating the iron and hammering while red-hot. During the forging process iron can be bent, flanges or other features introduced, or sheet metal produced.

Formation process

Any process that has affected the formation and development of the archaeological record. On a settlement site, for example, the nature of human occupation, the activities carried out, the pattern of breakage and loss of material, rubbish disposal, rebuilding or re-use of the same area will all influence the surviving archaeological deposits. After the site's abandonment, it will be further affected by such factors as erosion, glaciation, later agriculture, the activities of plants and animals as well as the natural processes of chemical action in the soil. The transformations to the archaeological data brought about by the former category of processes have been called cultural, those by the latter group non-cultural. To relate the observed evidence of an archaeological site to the human activity ultimately responsible for it, it is necessary to reconstruct these processes as fully as possible.

Fossil beach *see* RAISED BEACH

Frit
In the manufacture of glaze the oxides are normally suspended in water for application; however, some compounds, for example potassium and sodium, are very water soluble, and if applied direct would be absorbed into the pot. In many cases therefore, the raw materials are fused together under heat to form an insoluble glass known as frit. The frit is powdered, suspended in water and applied to the pot.

General systems theory
A theory which seeks the rules underlying the relationships observed in the real world, first developed by L. von Bertalanffy. The main concept used is the system, which consists of a number of elements and the relationships between them. In archaeological terms, the system might be the whole of a society's culture, or some part of it such as the economy or even a single settlement. The theory of systems is well developed; though the underlying mathematics have not proved applicable to archaeology, the systemic approach has been useful in concentrating attention on the relationships within a society. Systems can be regarded as either open or closed; the latter have no input of energy or matter from the outside, tend to reach a state of stable equilibrium in which small changes can be offset, and eventually stagnate and disintegrate, while open systems have an input of energy from the outside, reach a state of unstable equilibrium in which any small change can produce significant transformations in the system as a whole, and are characterized by growth and change. The process by which a system tends to maintain equilibrium in the face of changed surroundings is termed homeostasis, while morphogenesis is the process by which the structure is changed or elaborated. Some of these processes are cyclic, returning part of the energy expenditure to the system, in a process termed feedback; this is negative if it maintains stability, or positive if it promotes change. Systems incorporating positive feedback are of particular interest, since they can help to explain how an initial small change can lead to enormous consequences; in the origins of agriculture, for instance, an initial genetic change in wild grasses could have encouraged more intensive collection and cultivation, leading to still further genetic development, higher yields, population growth and yet more intensive cultivation. This cycle can be studied through the systemic relationship of the natural environment, subsistence economy and population.

Ghost wall *see* ROBBER TRENCH

Glaciation
The process by which land is covered by a glacier or ice-sheet; or the period of time during which such covering occurred. These periods of colder weather are also called glacials, and the warmer periods between them interglacials. At the onset of colder weather water was taken up into

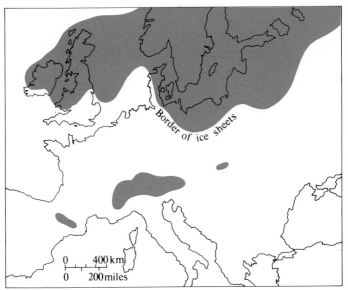

GLACIATION Above *The maximum extent of the ice during the last Glaciation, 70,000–10,000 BC.* Below *The correlation of the major stages during the Pleistocene period across the world. W = warm stage (interglacial); C = cold stage (glacial) (after Evans 1978).*

Britain	N.Europe	Alps	N.America	Others
w Flandrian				Post-glacial, Holocene
— 0.01 —				
c Devensian	Weichselian	Würm	Wisconsin	Last Glaciation
— 0.07 —				
w Ipswichian	Eemian		Sangamon	Last Interglacial
c Wolstonian	Saale	Riss	Illinoian	Penultimate Glaciation
w Hoxnian	Holstein		Yarmouth	Penultimate, Great Interglacial
c Anglian	Elster	Mindel	Kansan	Antepenultimate Glaciation
w Cromerian	Cromerian		Aftonian	Antepenultimate interglacial
— 0.45 —				
East Anglian Crags		Gunz	Nebraskan	Several alternate warm and cold stages
— 2.0 —				
Tertiary				

Periglacial features which can be confused in aerial photographs with archaeological site patterns: ice wedge polygons at Orton Longueville, Huntingdonshire, England.

the ice-sheets and glaciers, causing a drop in sea-level. Landscapes covered by ice can be recognized by the smooth rock surfaces and the U-shaped valleys formed by the ice-sheets and glaciers and the rocky rubble carried along in them. As the climate improved, the glaciers retreated, the ice melted and the sea-level rose. The ice deposited various forms of boulder clays, and banks of debris at the sides and ends of glaciers, known as moraines. Beyond the limits of glaciers and ice-sheets, extensive layers of outwash sands and gravels were deposited; where these deposits occur in lakes, they are called varves (q.v.). The effects of the climate which produced the glaciation were felt far beyond the limits of the ice; these periglacial features can be seen especially in the processes of erosion and deposition. Erosion was mainly brought about by solifluxion (q.v.); periglacial deposits, in addition to those due to solifluxion, include loess (q.v.) and coversands (q.v.). The low temperatures and the constant freezing and thawing have also affected the soil; these frost effects are called cryoturbation. Particularly characteristic are ice-wedges, polygonal cracks in the ground frequently recognizable in air-photographs. They were caused by the shrinking of the ground at low temperatures and the filling of the cracks with water, which subsequently expanded on freezing to open the crack still further.

The last two million years has been marked by a series of such glaciations. A scheme was originally worked out in central Europe, including four glacial phases, Gunz, Mindel, Riss and Würm. This was used for other areas of Europe, but it is now clear that the facts were much more complicated. Broad correlations between different parts of Europe and North America do nevertheless exist.

Glass layer counting
This technique was expected to be an accurate dating technique for glass, since it was thought that the layers present in the surface crust of ancient glass were added annually, and that counting them would yield a

chronometric date. While early results on glass of known date suggested that the method was accurate, subsequent research showed different numbers of layers on different parts of the same piece, and for some pieces of known date, not enough layers to suggest annual growth. An understanding of the processes which lead to the formation of the layers is necessary before the technique can be used with any confidence.

Ref.: NEWTON, R. G. 'The enigma of the layered crusts on some weathered glasses, a chronological account of the investigations', *Archaeometry* 13 (1971), 1–9.

Glaze

Glaze is a vitreous substance used to coat the surface of pottery. It is used for decoration, but also serves as an impermeable layer. Like glass, glaze is made from silica; this substance only melts at a temperature higher than that which would melt the pot, so a flux must be added to make it usable. Silica is present in most pottery, so in these cases only the flux—an oxide of sodium, lead or potassium—needs to be added, and a colourant if required, usually in the form of a frit (q.v.) crushed and suspended in water. The pot is then fired at a temperature suitable for melting the glaze (somewhere between 900°C and 1,200°C depending on the constituents), which runs into an even layer all over the pot.

Gloss

This form of surface treatment of pottery is frequently mistaken for glazing. In essence it involves the application of a slip (q.v.) to the surface, but the slip is made of very fine clay containing an unusually high proportion of the mineral illite, which results in a glossier, shinier surface than the normal slip after firing.

Grain impression

This term describes the occurrence of the impression of cereal grains in some form of artefact such as pottery. It occurs when clay is being worked in domestic surroundings and when grain lying around is accidentally incorporated into the clay. Its subsequent disintegration in firing leaves a mark of its presence in the clay, often in great detail. Before the widespread sieving and flotation (q.v.) of deposits began to yield large amounts of environmental evidence, these grain impressions were used to gain information on farming practices. Comparison with results from the sieving of deposits show grain impression evidence to be very biassed.

GRAIN IMPRESSION *The impression of a cereal grain in the clay of a Neolithic pot from Hurst Fen, Cambridgeshire, England.*

Granulation

An Etruscan gold fibula, 7th century BC, *from Vulci or Cerveteri. Fine* GRANULATION *covers the miniature sphinxes and lions that decorate its back and bow. Length 14 cm.*

A technique for the decoration of gold and silver work. Tiny spherical drops of metal, for example gold, were soldered on to a background, forming the required pattern. The drops may have been made by heating a gold wire until a drop formed, or by melting gold and slowly pouring it into cold water. As also for filigree (q.v.) the solder was normally a gold-copper alloy with a lower melting point than gold.

Graphite painting
This is a surface treatment for pottery involving the application of powdered graphite before firing. As for haematite coating (q.v.), the mineral may have been applied by mixing with a slip, or as a sort of paint. The resulting surface is silvery-grey and shiny.

Graver
A type of metalworking tool which comprises a number of subtypes, though all are hand-held, hard and sharp, and they cut away or engrave designs in metal objects. The round-nosed graver, with its curved edge, was frequently used for producing a curvilinear zigzag line, created by rolling the tool from side to side. This type of line is often erroneously called a rocked tracer line (tracer, q.v.), and it was a common form of decoration. A graver needs to be much harder than the metal on which it is used, and therefore for bronzeworking it should be of steel.

Ref.: LOWERY, R. P., SAVAGE, R. D. A. and WILKINS, R. L. 'Scriber, graver, scorper, tracer: notes on experiments in bronzeworking technique', *Proc. Prehist. Soc.* 37 (1971), 167–82.

Gravity model
A theory, derived from Newton's law of universal gravitation, that the degree of interaction between two communities is directly proportional to their populations and inversely proportional to the distance between them. Data from modern societies suggest that the model is valid for a wide range of types of interaction, such as migration, travel and communication. There are difficulties in its archaeological application, especially in the measurement of the size of a site, but it has been used to describe, for instance, the relationship of individual sites to rival production centres of obsidian, the proportion from any source varying with

its size and distance. The model can also be reformulated to give the 'breaking point' between two centres, that is the point at which the balance of interaction swings from one centre to the other. This can be used to predict, for example, the market territory dominated by each of a series of centres of different size, or to show the difference in area controlled by rival production centres of different size, for instance in the pottery industry.

Ref.: HODDER, I. and ORTON, C. *Spatial Analysis in Archaeology.* Cambridge, 1976, 187–95.

Grid method

A technique of excavation which used to be very popular but which is now used very sparingly, and only on particular types of site. It consists of laying out a regular series of square trenches with baulks in-between, each small square being suitable for excavation by two or three people. The main advantage of the method is that there are a large number of readily available sections on the site in the sides of the trenches. Other advantages are thought to be the ease of spoil removal (along the baulk) and the control which can be exercised over excavators. Particularly in areas of deep and complicated stratigraphy, the method can be used with considerable success, provided that the squares are of suitable size—they should not be less than three metres square—and are not too deep. On

Plan of an excavation at Williamsburg, Virginia, USA, carried out according to the GRID METHOD. *Note how many features and crucial stratigraphical relationships occur under the baulks (after Fagan 1972).*

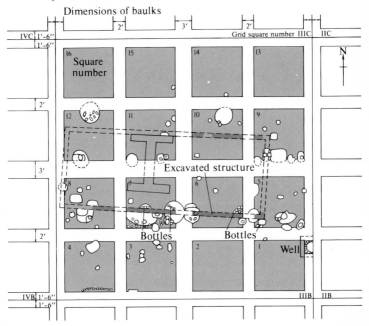

many sites, particularly open ones with little stratigraphy above the rock surface (however much there may be in pits or ditches), the method is wasteful of space and can be very misleading. On such a site large numbers of sections are unnecessary, since stratigraphy occurs mainly in deep features independent of each other which need no more than local sections. The baulks in the grid method may also obscure many of the important stratigraphical relationships, or make impossible the recognition of structures: in an area of ten three-metre squares with 600mm. baulks between the squares, about a quarter of the excavation area is under the baulk. In general this method of excavation is outmoded on all but complex, deeply stratified sites, and most open sites are now dug by area (area excavation, q.v.).

Grid planning
A technique for the planning of an archaeological site. It presupposes the presence of a measured grid on the site, and tapes running between the grid pegs of the square to be planned. The main piece of equipment is a rigid framed grid, normally one metre square, strung at 100mm. intervals. At the beginning of the planning of a square this grid would be laid flat on the ground at one of the corners. The draughtsman stands over it and transfers the information seen on the ground direct to the paper, at scale: the edge of a pit, running through the edge of several 100mm. squares, can be instantly recorded on squared paper. The metre grid is then moved along one side of the square to the next position, and the process is repeated, using a tape between the two side tapes to ensure accurate placing of the frame. This planning technique allows the fast recording of very large areas, but is not as accurate as triangulation (q.v.) for the pinpointing of small objects and features, since the view of the draughtsman is not always totally vertical. The use of grid planning and triangulation together satisfies most of the combined needs of speed and accuracy.

Grog
Fragments of old or wasted pottery which are ground up and added to clay as filler material to help reduce plasticity.

Haematite coating
A surface treatment for pottery involving the application of powdered haematite iron ore before firing. Possible methods of application are various: it may have been mixed with a slip (q.v.) and then applied, or painted on as a suspension in water. When fired the surface normally appears red, although under reduced firing conditions it may turn black.

Half-life
The time taken for half of a given amount of a radioactive substance to decay into a non-radioactive substance. If a sample, such as a piece of wood, has half of the original amount of radiocarbon remaining, then a time equivalent to the half-life has passed since it died. The half-life of

radiocarbon is 5730 ± 40 years, while the half-life of radioactive potassium, used in potassium-argon dating (q.v.), is 1.3 billion years.

Hardness

This term refers to the measured hardness of substances such as metal or
glass. There are scales of hardness, and tests have been devised to measure
this aspect so that, for example, the efficiency of two types of metal under
stress can be compared. Among available scales or tests of hardness are
the Moh scale using specific minerals numbered in order of hardness with
which other substances are compared; the diamond pyramid scale; and
the Brinell hardness scale, perhaps the most commonly used in archaeological contexts. This test method involves the forcing of a ball of
hardened steel of known diameter into the sample to be tested, for a
standard length of time under standard pressure: the softer the metal
under test, the greater the diameter of the resulting depression, which is
measured with a micrometer. Such tests allow conclusions to be drawn
about past metalworking techniques and their efficiency.

Heavy mineral analysis

A method used particularly in the examination of pottery in order to
determine the geological source of the sand inclusions in the clay of the
pot, and therefore the probable area of manufacture. The method
involves the crushing of 10–30g. of pot and the floating of the resulting

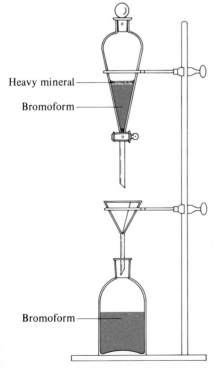

Heavy mineral

Bromoform

Bromoform

HEAVY MINERAL ANALYSIS *The
apparatus required for the
separation of heavy minerals
using, for example, bromoform
(after Cornwall 1958).*

powder on a heavy liquid such as bromoform with a specific gravity of 2.9. The heavy minerals like zircon, garnet and tourmaline sink, while the quartz sand and clay float: it is the heavy minerals (separated, identified and counted under a microscope) which characterize the parent formation, and which enable the source of the sand to be identified. While for Britain much information about the distribution of heavy minerals is available, in other parts of the world the geological data are not detailed enough to make the identification of sources universally easy.

Ref.: PEACOCK, D. P. S. 'The scientific analysis of ancient ceramics: a review', *World Archaeology* I (1970), 375–89.

Hierarchy
The organization of any group of items into a series of classes ranked from high to low, each successively higher class having fewer members. In a social hierarchy, the ranking would reflect differences in power, prestige or access to economic resources. In a settlement hierarchy, the individual sites might be organized on the basis of population size or number of functions fulfilled into a series of classes such as town, village, hamlet.

HIERARCHY *Design of hierarchical tribal structure showing stages in the system (after Sahlins 1968).*

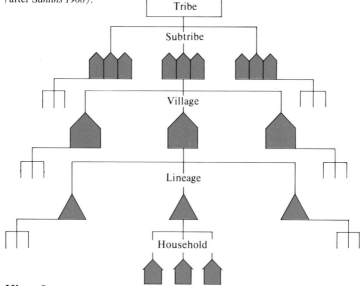

Hinge fracture
A feature of a struck flint flake which occurs either through a fault in striking technique or through the nature of a particular piece of flint. Instead of coming to a sharp, thin end, the struck flake ends in a rounded, turned-out edge, suggesting secondary working (q.v.) or polishing which may never have occurred.

Histogram

A method of visually representing 'the frequency of different measured values of one continuous numeric attribute' (Doran and Hodson, *op. cit.* p. 123). If measurements of length have been taken for bronze spearheads from one particular area and period, for example, the measurements are represented by marking off intervals of lengths on the horizontal axis, and counting the number of spearheads falling into each division. These numbers are marked off on the vertical axis. The main problem is deciding on the number of divisions to be made, though in practice it usually resolves itself reasonably easily. In order to compare one set of data with

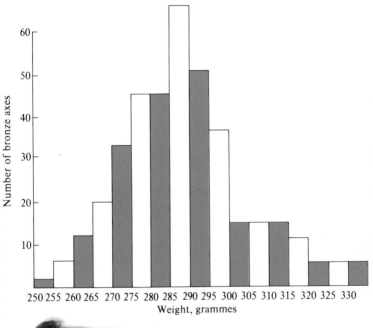

HISTOGRAM *A histogram showing the dispersion of 320 Breton Late Bronze Age socketed axes in terms of their weight (*after *Briard 1965). A Breton socketed axe, unprovenanced, of the kind measured for the histogram.*

another, or others, a cumulative version of the histogram may be used, where the succeeding values are added to the preceding: these are called cumulative frequency polygons, and are useful for comparative work, but are difficult to use if single histograms need to be extracted.

Ref.: DORAN, J. E. and HODSON, F. R. *Mathematics and Computers in Archaeology*. London, 1975, 121–9.

Horizon

A phase, characterized by a particular artefact or monument type, which can be recognized over a wide area and which may cross cultural boundaries. The horizon marker, for example a type of pot, appears within a short space of time all over a region, and thus it is assumed that the cultures in which it occurs are contemporary. The term is less commonly used now that chronometric dating techniques allow accurate local chronologies to be built up, and when different forms of explanation are used for the appearance of such types.

Household cluster

A term used in American archaeology to describe a set of features associated with one house structure. The components would be a house, a few storage pits, graves, a rubbish area, perhaps an oven, and activity areas (q.v.).

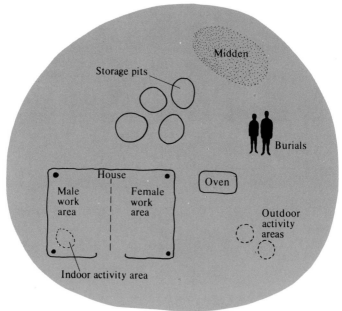

An idealized typical HOUSEHOLD CLUSTER *(after Flannery 1976).*

Independent invention

A theory that maintains the likelihood of new ideas, such as the invention of copper and iron working, or the erection of particular types of monumental building, being invented in more than one place at the same or different times, thus denying the theory of diffusion (q.v.) as the single possible explanation. New chronometric dating techniques have shown the probability of independent invention for at least some of these ideas. Theoretically, if two different cultures have reached a similar technological level, there is no reason why both could not take a further step in the same direction quite independently.

Indirect percussion

A method of removing flakes from a flint core which causes less wasteful shatter of the material than direct percussion (q.v.). The hammer or hammerstone does not strike the flint but a wooden or bone punch, usually with a prepared edge, which is pressed on the flint, so that the manufacture of flakes is more controlled.

The INDIRECT PERCUSSION *method of flaking flint and stone (*after *Oakley 1972).*

Induced polarization technique

A technique used for the location of archaeological features which has many similarities with resistivity surveying (q.v.). It involves the measurement of transient induced polarization voltage which results from the passing of direct current through the ground via electrodes. The method requires the presence of an electrolytic solution, and thus it is the greater or lesser water content of the features, in contrast to the surrounding soil, that allows their detection. A ditch will have a high induced polarization response, while a wall will have a low one.

Ref.: ASPINALL, A. and LYNAM, J. T. 'An induced polarisation instrument for the detection of near surface features', *Prospezioni Archeologiche* 5 (1970), 67–75.

Industry

This term defines a set of artefacts which are thought to be the product of a single group or society because of the constant recurrence of specific types. The term is restricted to groups of a single class of artefact, such as pottery or flint, for example the Mousterian flint industry. A group of industries occurring frequently in association may indicate a culture (q.v.) which has, however, more aspects than simply its technological industries.

Infra-red absorption spectrometry

A technique used to identify minerals and chemical compounds in artefacts, either to determine their nature or to help with the identification of their source. A small sample is taken from the object and is ground finely before being subjected to infra-red radiation. Constituent atoms in

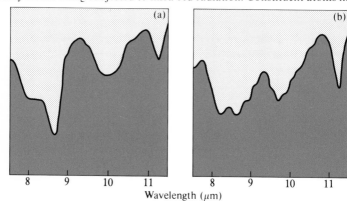

INFRARED ABSORPTION SPECTROMETRY *The infrared absorption spectra for* a. *Baltic and* b. *Sicilian amber, showing that they can be distinguished (after Beck et al 1965). Left An amber necklace from Derrybrien, Co. Galway, Ireland. Diameter 30 cm.*

the specimen vibrate at characteristic frequencies; if the frequency is the same as that of the radiation, the radiation will be absorbed, while if frequencies do not match, the radiation will pass through the sample. A measurement of the amount of absorption at each wavelength leads to the identification of the minerals and chemical compounds present. Though the method can be used for both inorganic and organic materials, it tends to be used alongside X-ray diffraction for inorganic substances, where it is more sensitive to poorly crystallized minerals; it is particularly useful, however, for organic materials such as amber, where contrasting spectra have led to the identification of sources.

Ref.: TITE, M. S. *Methods of Physical Examination in Archaeology.* London, 1972, 288–91.

Insect analysis

A technique used in attempts to reconstruct past environments. With pollen analysis (q.v.) and molluscan analysis (q.v.) it can reveal information on climate, the environment and, occasionally, the activities of man. Insect remains are usually found in the form of the exoskeleton, parts such as the wing-cases of beetles, and they always come from anaerobic deposits such as ditches, wells, pits and peat bogs. They are separated from the soil sample by flotation (q.v.), though normally under strict control in a laboratory rather than by on-site machine flotation.

INSECT ANALYSIS *A scanning electron micrograph of* Monotoma spinicollis, *a denizen of rotting plants, found at York, and a good example of the type of insect remains that can be recovered from archaeological deposits.*

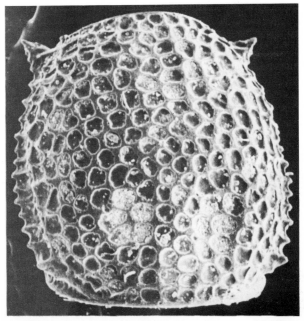

Good comparative material is necessary for identification purposes, though many of the parts of insects that are species-distinctive do not survive in archaeological deposits. Insects respond more quickly than plants to climatic change, and may therefore assist in the identification of micro-climatic phases; they also have habitat preferences, and can help to identify specific environmental situations. Certain beetles only eat specific plants, and thus their presence can point to the plant species at an extremely local level. Other insects are found in particular environments associated with man, such as dung beetles, furniture beetles, grain beetles and beetles associated with the tanning of leather. It has therefore been possible on some sites to assign specific functions to structures through the analysis of the insect remains.

Ref.: COOPE, G. R. 'The value of Quaternary insect faunas in the interpretation of ancient ecology and climate', in *Quaternary Palaeoecology.* ed. E. J. Cushing and H. E. Wright. London, 1967, 359–80.

Isostasy

This term defines changes in the height of the land in relation to the sea. Though these variations are not necessarily associated with changes in sea-level (eustasy, q.v.), a major event such as glaciation can affect both land and sea. The weight of ice sheets can cause a lowering in the height of the land, but a thaw at the end of a glaciation frees the land of this pressure and it rises.

Lacquer

A varnishing substance used from prehistoric times in the areas where it was first developed. The basis for the varnish is, in many cases, lac, the sap of *Rhus vernicifera.* which is cleaned of impurities and used without further treatment. In other areas the basis of lacquer is the gummy deposit secreted by the insect *Coccus lacca.* Imitations of these substances by solutions of resin or gum in turpentine come later. Lacquer reaches its maximum hardness in a moist atmosphere.

Landnam

A Danish word meaning 'land-taking', used to describe a common form of early agriculture in which an area of woodland was cleared and cultivated. It was later abandoned and was taken over by weeds, finally reverting to woodland. Its regeneration began with the birch, a rapid colonizer of areas cleared by fire. This 'landnam' was recognized in pollen analysis by changes in the pollen spectra: the drop in tree pollen, the appearance of cereal pollens and those of weeds of cultivation (q.v.), a subsequent increase in the latter and an eventual reappearance of birch. This 'landnam' recognizable in the pollen record clearly represents the slash-and-burn cultivation (q.v.) so common among early farmers.

Lead bronze

An alloy of copper and tin with lead, often having as much as 10% lead. The presence of lead, which remains free in the alloy as opposed to becoming part of the crystalline structure, increases the fluidity of the metal in its molten state, and makes the casting of finely detailed objects easier. It does, however, have a softening effect, and therefore lead bronze is less suitable for a cutting edge.

Lead isotope analysis

The relative abundance of lead isotopes differs according to the origin of the lead, and it should therefore be possible to pinpoint the source of a piece of lead once the ratios of the isotopes have been determined.

A mass spectrometer is used on a small sample to determine the ratio of the isotopic concentrations, which are similar in different regions if the geological time scale is similar. Since the ratios do not change whatever process is undergone by the artefact, the method can be used to identify sources of lead impurities in other metals as well as in glass and glaze.

Ref.: BRILL, R. H. 'Lead and oxygen isotopes in ancient objects', *Philos. Trans. Royal Soc. London* A269 (1970), 143–64.

Level

An instrument which takes vertical measurements in surveying procedures, and which is much used in excavation for the recording of site contours and accurate depths of features. There are several types of levelling instrument, the Y or dumpy level, the tilting level and the self-levelling level. They all consist of a telescopic sight mounted on a tripod, with a variety of spirit levels to help level the instrument. The differences between the types are in the ease of levelling: the first has a single spirit level for the whole instrument, the second a separate spirit level for spindle

How a LEVEL *is used to take readings of height and depth on an excavation.*

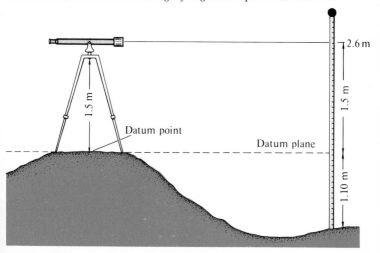

and telescope with a tilting mechanism and adjustable screw on the telescope, and the third an optical part operated by a pendulum so that the line of sight is always horizontal. Having established a datum point (q.v.), the instrument is sighted on a levelling staff or rod which is marked in a graduated scale, metric or imperial. The difference in level between the telescope and the base of the rod can be read off on this scale, and the result subtracted from the height of the level itself above ground; the final figure gives the real height, or depth, of the feature above or below the ground at instrument point. A series of levels taken across a site will give contours, while excavated features and small finds (q.v.) can be levelled in with greater accuracy than with tapes from a hypothetical ground surface. All sections (q.v.) should also be levelled in.

Linear regression analysis

A statistical procedure for determining the relationship between two variables. It has many applications in archaeology, for example the study of variations in population or the size of clay-pipe stems through time, or the relationship between the quantity of an item and the distance from its source. One variable (e.g. time or distance) is regarded as independent, while the second is dependent on it; from a set of known observations, it is possible to estimate the relationship between the two. Thus, given the population figures for different times in a region, it would be possible to predict the population for any other date. The method assumes that there is a linear relationship between the variables, and uses only one variable to explain all the variation in the other; these can be serious limitations.

Locational analysis

A set of techniques borrowed from geography to study the relationships between sites and between a site and its environment. Many such techniques have been developed in geography, and some have been found particularly useful by archaeologists. The relationship between sites can be examined in different ways: the degree of clustering in the sites can be measured by nearest-neighbour analysis (q.v.), and the complexity of the communication system between them by network analysis (q.v.). For the emergence of a hierarchy of sites of different status, the rank-size rule (q.v.) is used, while the spatial arrangement of sites of different status may be explored by the use of central place theory (q.v.). There are other methods for looking at the location of an individual site in its environment; site catchment analysis (q.v.) is an archaeological technique for measuring the resources available to a site. It is based on the principle of least effort, which holds that a site will theoretically be located where the total energy expenditure of the inhabitants will be minimized. Thus for an industrial site the location will be chosen in view of the relative costs of transporting the raw materials and the finished products; if the materials are bulky, the site will be placed near to their source, but if the product is comparative, heavy or valuable, it may be nearer to the market. Similarly for an agricultural site, the settlement and its environment will be organized so that those areas such as arable fields which need the most attention and effort will be nearest, while those such as occasional pasture will be furthest from the settlement. Thus, if the nature of the raw materials or the soils are known, it would be possible to predict the theoretical locations for sites; if the locations and environment are known, the nature of the exploitation of the resources can be predicted.

Loess
One of the wind-blown sediments, silt, which is derived from glacial deposits and is carried hundreds of kilometres before its deposition. Because of its exceptional fertility areas of loess were especially chosen for settlement by early agriculturists; in Central and Eastern Europe, as well as North America, there are notable concentrations of sites on loess.

Lynchet
A feature of the agricultural landscape caused by ploughing. Field boundaries, such as banks or walls, become enlarged and overlain by hillwash material loosened by the cultivation process, which builds up against them. A corresponding erosion from the downslope side of the boundary forms a negative lynchet. Although hillwash itself is a natural process, the loosening of the soil and the original field boundaries were created by human agency, and the appearance of lynchets is a classic marker of agriculture.

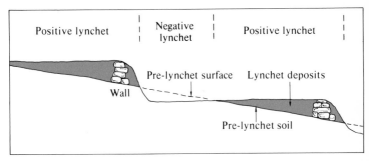

The formation of positive and negative LYNCHETS *(after* Evans 1978*).*

Macroband
A term of modern anthropology used to describe a group of several, usually related families who set up seasonal camps from which they carry out hunter-gatherer activities. There can be more than one camp in the region exploited by each macroband, which moves from one area to another in order to exploit seasonal food resources. At some times of the year the macroband splits into microbands (q.v.). The macroband is suggested as a model for prehistoric hunter-gatherer societies.

Magnetic dating
A theoretically chronometric dating technique which uses the thermo-

remanent magnetism of certain types of archaeological material, and the fact that changes are known to have taken place in the direction and intensity of the earth's magnetic field. Magnetic minerals like haematite and magnetite are present in clay and rocks: each grain has its own magnetic orientation. When heated to the so-called blocking temperature, the original magnetic orientation of the particles is destroyed, and they will take on the orientation of the earth's magnetic field in a fixed alignment which does not alter after cooling. Errors can arise if the sample is moved after firing, since the method must assume that the direction is the same as it was when fired: thus the method cannot be used for portable material like pottery, but is suitable for kilns and hearths. Other possible sources of error are the possibility of refiring being unnoticed in excavation, or the acquisition of magnetism through chemical changes.

The sample, which must be kept clean and unbroken, is encased in plaster before removal, and the exact orientation is marked on before it is lifted; this procedure is very time-consuming. The measurements are made in the laboratory using a parastatic or other magnetometer. Once the direction of the archaeological sample has been determined, it may be possible to date it by fitting it to the secular variation curve established for the local area. There is no universal curve, since not only the earth's main field varies, but there are also local disturbances. Since the dating of the curve has to be constructed through independent dating techniques, and

MAGNETIC DATING *The variations in the location of the magnetic pole since AD 1, one of the factors affecting the changes in magnetic orientation* (after *Weaver 1967*).

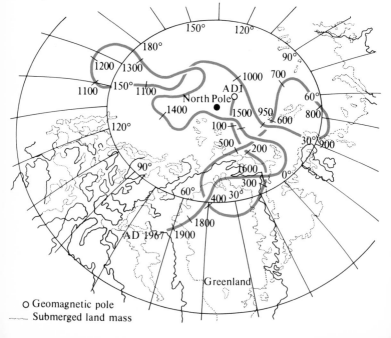

o Geomagnetic pole
---- Submerged land mass

these are not available for every area, there are not established curves for every region: indeed, the scientists seek well-dated examples of suitable material in order to establish the local curves. As a dating technique therefore, it is strictly limited to those areas where dated curves have been established.

A more recent dating technique using thermo-remanent magnetism is palaeointensity dating (also known as archaeomagnetic intensity dating). The principle here is that the thermo-remanent magnetism in burnt clay is proportional to the intensity of the magnetic field acting on the clay as it cools down. The measurement of its intensity, and a comparison with the intensity revealed by reheating in today's magnetic field, gives a ratio for the past and present fields which can be used to establish a curve of the variation in the earth's magnetic field intensity. The method promises to be more useful for chronometric dating (q.v.) when experimental procedures have been refined, since direction *in situ* is not required and it can therefore be used for pottery and other artefacts as well as hearths and kilns.

Ref.: TITE, M. S. *Methods of Physical Examination in Archaeology.* London, 1972, 134–50.

BUCHA, V. *et al.* 'Geomagnetic intensity: changes during the past 3,000 years in the Western Hemisphere', *Science* 168 (1970), 111–14.

Magnetic surveying

A technique for the location of archaeological features adapted from techniques used in geological surveying. It is based on the fact that features with thermo-remanent magnetism, like hearths or kilns, or features with a high humus content, like pits or ditches, and iron objects, distort the earth's magnetic field from the normal. Instruments such as the proton magnetometer (q.v.) or the differential fluxgate gradiometer (q.v.) are used to measure these disturbances, and by plotting the results a map of the features located can be built up. The ways in which the different types of feature distort the magnetic field vary, though they can all be picked up on the same instrument. Haematite or magnetite, present in most clays, have a small magnetic effect when unburnt, since the grains point in random directions and cancel each other out. Once heated to about 700°C or more, the grains line up, increasing the magnetic effect and causing an anomaly in the magnetic field. This thermo-remanent magnetism is also the basis for magnetic dating (q.v.). Anomalies caused by ditches and pits occur because of what is called the susceptibility of the filling. The magnetic susceptibility is the amount of magnetization which can be induced by placing a sample in a magnetic field; the filling of a ditch or a pit has greater susceptibility than the surrounding area because of higher humus content and perhaps the presence of burnt occupation material. On the basis that contrast between feature and surroundings locates the features, walls and other stone settings can also be located since they have less susceptibility than the area around them, i.e. they exhibit a reverse anomaly.

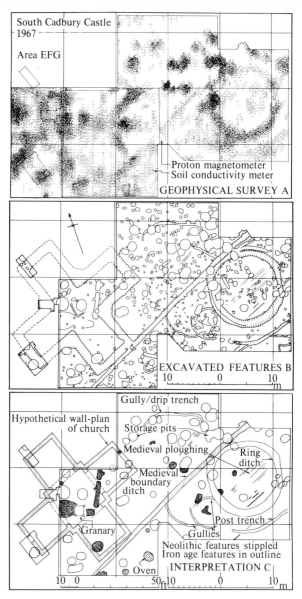

Area EFG

South Cadbury Castle
1967

Proton magnetometer
Soil conductivity meter

GEOPHYSICAL SURVEY A

EXCAVATED FEATURES B

10   0   10
m

Hypothetical wall-plan
of church

Gully/drip trench

Storage pits

Medieval ploughing

Medieval
boundary
ditch

Ring
ditch

Granary

Gullies

Post trench

Neolithic features stippled
Iron age features in outline

Oven

INTERPRETATION C

10 0   50 10   0   10
ft   m

MAGNETIC SURVEYING *The results produced by pre-excavation survey at South Cadbury, Somerset, England, and a plan and interpretation of the excavated features for comparison (*after *Alcock 1968).*

The presence of modern iron features such as wire fences can cause problems with this technique of location; if the area to be surveyed is clearly crossed with power lines or fenced with iron posts, a resistivity survey (q.v.) may be more suitable. The method of surveying used requires a grid to be measured out on the site and readings to be taken at regular intervals. The nature of the site may prevent such a grid being laid out, for instance if it is heavily wooded, and magnetic survey may not be possible on these sites. The method of presentation of the data varies with the operator, though most will produce a pictorial representation for the archaeologist, as well as the numerical readings initially acquired. On occasion, plans made from magnetic surveys are so close to what was eventually found in excavation that in future it may not be necessary, on a site with ideal conditions, to excavate the total area in order to understand the whole ground plan.

Ref.: TITE, M. S. *Methods of Physical Examination in Archaeology.* London, 1972, 9–25.

Magnetic susceptibility *see* MAGNETIC SURVEYING

Market
A form of exchange in which the price of a commodity is fixed by the relative proportions of supply and demand. The term may also be applied more specifically to the place where people come together for transactions of this sort, or the occasion on which they do so, though it is not necessary for people actually to meet together for the market principle to operate. Though a degree of social control is necessary, for instance to guarantee access to the market and the security of traders, it does not extend to the regulation of trade, and prices are fixed independently. The system favours the emergence of a single price, though it fluctuates through time.

Melting
The point at which melting of a metal occurs is that where the metal liquefies. This point must be reached if a metal object is to be cast, and therefore good temperature control of the furnace is essential. In antiquity gold, silver, copper and lead were all melted and cast, but the melting and thus casting of iron was not achieved until the medieval period. Melting points are as follows: tin, $232°C$; lead, $327°C$; silver, $960°C$; gold, $1,063°C$; copper, $1,083°C$; iron $1,525°C$.

Metallographic microscopy
The microscopic examination of metal artefacts is carried out with the aim of studying the techniques involved in their manufacture rather than their composition. A sample is taken from the artefact (in ideal circumstances this would be a cross-section slice, but this is usually too destructive), and is highly polished. The surface is then etched in order to dissolve some of the metal, leaving visible its internal structure for examination under a metallurgical microscope. This uses reflected light which emphasizes the uneven surfaces revealed by the etching process and caused by such

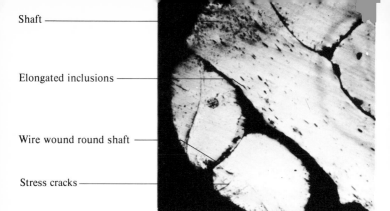

Shaft

Elongated inclusions

Wire wound round shaft

Stress cracks

METALLOGRAPHIC MICROSCOPY *A section through a brass pinhead, 16th to 18th century* AD, *with details revealed by the microscope. The elongated inclusions in the shaft suggest wire-drawing; the distortion of the top of the shaft and of the wires wound round the head show that the wires were forced on tightly by stamping, which has also caused stress cracks. Mag.* × *40.*

features as the boundaries between grains of metal. The size and shape of the grains or dendrites in a metal, as well as other details of microstructure, can yield information on casting methods or post-casting working. The technique can be used on both ferrous and non-ferrous metals.

Ref.: SHRAGER, A. M. *Elementary Metallurgy and Metallography.* New York, 1961.

Microband
This modern anthropological term describes a very small band of a few people, perhaps a single family, who carry out collecting and hunting activities together seasonally, and who may belong to a macroband (q.v.) which they rejoin at other seasons of the year for greater efficiency when there is a glut of seasonal food.

Millefiore
A technique of glassworking which takes its name from the flower-like decoration it produces. The technique can be carried out in more than one way. One method is to take a cane of glass, encase it with several layers of glass of different colours, and then heat the whole and roll it on a corrugated surface, thus compressing the colours at certain points and producing a rod with a flower-like section. Small slices can be cut off this rod and inlaid into the object to be decorated. Alternatively, thin glass rods of different colours can be laid together into a pattern, fused together, drawn out and cut in slices in the same way.

Model
An idealized representation of the real world, used to demonstrate a simplified version of some of its characteristics. Such models vary greatly in nature and in the degree of abstraction; as a model becomes more

abstract and loses specific information about the real world, so it becomes more general in application. At the most realistic and least general level, it might be a physical model of a site or landscape to explain some feature of its function or organization; such models at full scale are well known in experimental archaeology (q.v.). The term is more frequently used for theoretical models, which again vary greatly. At their simplest, a map showing, for example, the distribution of sites in a region or a scatter diagram (q.v.) showing the relationship between two measured variables could be regarded as models; they can then be made more general by transforming them mathematically, for instance by linear regression analysis (q.v.) or trend surface analysis (q.v.). The models need not be based on specific archaeological data, but can be derived from a number of sources: invented data can be generated by computer simulation (q.v.); geometrical and mathematical models can also be used, such as central place theory (q.v.) or the rank-size rule (q.v.) in the study of regional settlement, or catastrophe theory (q.v.) in the study of cultural collapse. General systems theory (q.v.) can also be a fruitful source of systems models designed to show a simplified version of the working of a complex social or economic organization. The term model can also be used in a less specific sense for any general mode of thought in which archaeological research is conducted, for example descriptive, historical or ecological.

Molluscan analysis

The analysis of molluscan remains, of both marine and land species, as part of the examination of the environment of man. Edible species also yield information on the subsistence economy of certain groups. In most cases it is the shells which survive, though even these may disappear if the immediate environment is not calcareous. The analysis of marine mollusca involves separation of the shells from the sample by wet sieving (q.v.), and the identification of varieties. This leads not only to information about past environments, since the molluscs prefer particular habitats, but also to assumptions about the exploitation of these resources by man. Frequently the occurrence of mounds of discarded shell debris (shell middens) allows a clear understanding of the collecting patterns,

MOLLUSCAN ANALYSIS Overleaf
A diagram of molluscan remains from Pitstone, Buckinghamshire, England, showing the changes in molluscan population which reflect changes in the environment (after Evans 1972).
Left *A sample of the types of land-snails which can be recovered and identified from archaeological deposits:*
a. Helix pomatia;
b. Helix aspersa;
c. Pomatias elegans;
d. Discus rotundatus;
e. Cochlicopa lubrica.

75

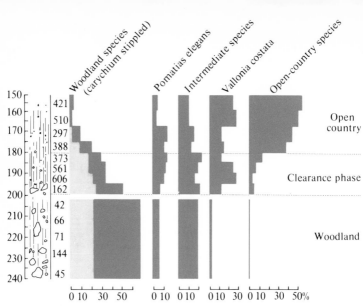

seasonal use and preferences of man in the marine region. Land snails are increasingly used as an adjunct to pollen and insect analysis in attempts to reconstruct past environments. Samples are wet-sieved, dried and identified; again, many types of land snail have definite preferences for certain habitats, and it is possible to identify, for example, woodland species and open-country species which, if they followed each other in a stratigraphical sequence on a site might suggest a clearance of the land. Snail diagrams are presented like pollen diagrams with percentages of species appearing in the samples. Changes visible in these diagrams may not only mean environmental change but also climatic change.

Ref.: EVANS, J. G. *Land Snails in Archaeology.* London, 1972.

Mössbauer spectroscopy
The use of this method of physical analysis has been confined mainly to the examination of iron compounds, though other uses have been suggested. The Mössbauer effect of recoil-free emission and absorption of gamma rays only occurs with a limited number of isotopes, of which one of the iron isotopes is useful in archaeological contexts. The specimen, which is frequently pottery, is subjected to a bombardment of gamma rays; the amount of absorption by the iron nuclei is measured, and this yields information both on the presence of iron-bearing minerals in the clay, and on the conditions of firing during manufacture. Because of its sensitivity to short-range crystalline order, the technique is better for examining poorly crystallized iron-bearing minerals than X-ray diffraction.

Ref.: WERTHEIM, G. K. *Mössbauer Effect: Principles and Applications.* New York, 1964.

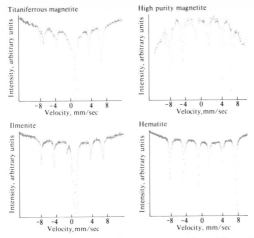

MÖSSBAUER SPECTROSCOPY *The Mössbauer spectra of four different iron ore types showing how they can be distinguished (after Flannery 1976).*

Munsell Soil Colour Charts

This aid is used in the physical examination and recording of objects where colour is felt to be an essential or at least a significant aspect of the analysis. Devised by A. Munsell specifically for use with soil colour, the three factors of hue, value and chroma are taken into consideration, all rated on a scale of 0–10 and therefore expressed quantitatively. Hue describes the colours of the spectrum present, value their concentration and chroma their purity. The colour of soil or, for example, pottery, can be matched in the chart and given a value, so that anyone with a similar set of charts can see the exact colour of the material. The method allows direct comparison of colours without physically moving the material around, and is clearly preferable to the use of such descriptions as 'reddish-brown' or 'yellowish-grey'.

Nearest-neighbour analysis

A method of analysing the degree of dispersion in a distribution pattern, first developed by plant ecologists studying the concentration of certain species. A nearest-neighbour index (usually denoted by the symbol R), is calculated from the ratio of the average observed distance from each point in the pattern to its nearest neighbour, to the average distance expected if the pattern were randomly distributed, which depends solely on the density of the pattern being studied. The index R varies from 0.00 for a totally clustered pattern through 1.00 for a random distribution to a maximum of 2.15 for a completely regularly spaced pattern. The index is influenced by the size of the study area chosen, since any pattern will appear more or less clustered as the area around it increases or decreases;

it is therefore essential to select a relevant framework for the distribution being studied. With any boundary, however, it is possible for the index to be distorted by the 'boundary effect' to give a figure closer to the maximum than would be justified; this arises because the nearest neighbours of points near to the boundary may in fact lie beyond the boundary and hence not be properly counted, thus increasing the figure for the observed mean distance. It is also essential that the points in the pattern being analysed are of the same date and similar function, and that the pattern should be complete. The index R describes only a part of the total pattern and can serve as a useful basis for asking more detailed questions about the factors that underlie the observed pattern.

Ref.: HODDER, I. and ORTON, C. *Spatial Analysis in Archaeology.* London, 1976, 38–51.

Network analysis

The study of any network or system of links and nodes, especially a communication system such as roads. Attention is paid to the way in which the network is organized rather than to the actual lengths of the links. It is possible to study the degree to which an efficient system has been evolved; Roman roads, for instance, are particularly suitable for this sort of analysis, and the changing patterns demanded by military and civilian usage can be distinguished.

Neutron activation analysis

This is a physical method of analysis used to determine the chemical composition of various substances. It can be totally non-destructive of the sample, and can be used on a wide variety of materials such as flint, obsidian, pottery, coins, faience, etc. It is somewhat different in principle from the other physical methods of chemical analysis (optical emission spectrometry, q.v.; atomic absorption spectrometry, q.v.; X-ray fluorescence spectrometry, q.v.), since it involves the excitation of the atomic nuclei rather than the atomic electrons. The specimen is placed in a metal receptacle large enough to accommodate small specimens whole (though large artefacts must be sampled, a weight of 50–100mg. being required), and is subjected to a bombardment of neutrons, which interact with the atomic nuclei of the elements present in the sample, forming radioactive isotopes. These decay, emitting gamma rays whose energies are characteristic of the particular element which has been excited. The gamma rays are detected by a scintillation or semiconductor counter, and a determination of their energies allows the identification of the constituent elements; the concentration of these elements can be estimated from the intensity of the gamma rays at a particular energy. The time between the neutron activation of the sample and the measurement of the gamma rays depends on the half-lives (q.v.) of the radioactive isotopes, which may range from seconds to thousands of years: often a few weeks may be necessary before measurement takes place. Neutron activation analysis has an advantage over X-ray fluorescence spectrometry since it analyses the whole specimen

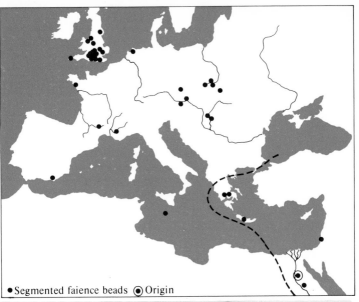

● Segmented faience beads ◉ Origin

NEUTRON ACTIVATION ANALYSIS *Map showing the distribution of segmented faience beads in Europe (*after *Fagan 1972).*

A necklace from a Bronze Age grave at Upton Lovell, Wiltshire, with faience beads of segmented and quoit shape, as well as amber and shale.

as opposed to the surface only; it, too, can be non-destructive, but care has to be taken that the neutron dose is not so great as to make the specimen unsafe for handling through radioactivity. Rapid analytical procedures are possible, and the method is particularly useful for the identification of trace elements; however, it is not universally applicable since some elements have too short a half-life for measurement, and others do not form radioactive isotopes.

Ref.: TITE, M. S. *Methods of Physical Examination in Archaeology.* London, 1972, 273–8.

Niello
A black substance which was used to inlay patterns in silver. There are various types of composition of the material, the most common being a mixture of copper and silver sulphides, though lead was sometimes used. The material was soft; it was cast into the cut-out pattern on the object and polished flat.

Nitrogen test
A method of chemical analysis of bone to establish its date relative to others in the same or neighbouring deposits. Nitrogen is present in bone in a proportion of approximately 4%; this percentage declines after burial in the ground at a slow uniform rate, and therefore the results of chemical analysis can show by how much the nitrogen content has declined. Since the rate of decline is affected by local environmental factors such as temperature or chemical constituents in the find deposit, only relative dates for bones for particular areas can be established. However, the high nitrogen content of the Piltdown jawbone was enough to show clearly that the bone was modern and a hoax.

The Piltdown skull, the jawbone of which was found to be of recent date as a result of NITROGEN TESTS.

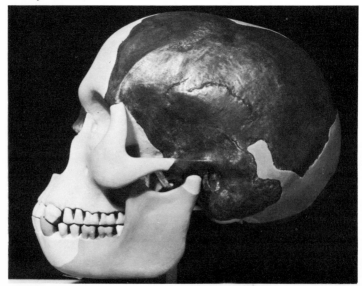

Ref.: OAKLEY, K. P. 'Analytical methods of dating bones', in *Science in Archaeology.* ed. D. Brothwell and E. Higgs. 2nd ed. London, 1969, 35–45.

Numerical taxonomy

A set of mathematical procedures for grouping individual items into classes. Much archaeological effort is devoted to classification, and the development of numerical methods has greatly clarified the steps involved in such a process and brought a new level of objectivity to it. The technique used is cluster analysis, which produces groupings of items based on their degree of similarity. There are different ways of measuring the similarity between items, and different techniques of producing clusters from such measurements. Agglomerative techniques start with the most similar items and repeatedly add new members to existing clusters as the standard of similarity is lowered; divisive methods, on the other hand, start with the entire collection to be classified and repeatedly subdivide into smaller groups on the basis of certain attributes. The

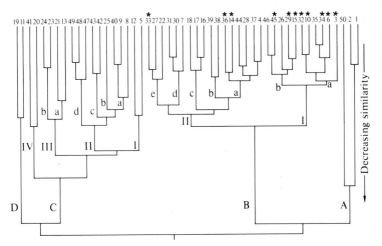

NUMERICAL TAXONOMY *Above A cluster analysis of 50 Upper Palaeolithic assemblages: an exercise in numerical taxonomy (after Hodson 1969–70). **Below** A split-based bone point from La Ferrassie, Dordogne, France, of the type found in the assemblages analysed (after Bordes 1968).*

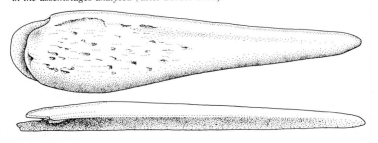

results of the analyses can be shown in the form of a dendrogram (q.v.), but the interpretation of the groupings produced will depend on a detailed assessment of the archaeological data itself.

Obsidian hydration layer dating

A method of dating obsidian artefacts by measuring the thickness of the hydration layer found on the surface. The surface of obsidian starts to absorb water as soon as it is exposed by flaking during manufacture of an artefact. As the process continues at a constant rate, the thickness of the layer as compared with that in obsidian artefacts of a known date will suggest the amount of time since manufacture. The layer of hydrated

OBSIDIAN HYDRATION DATING *The hydration layer in an obsidian artefact viewed in ordinary and polarised light.*

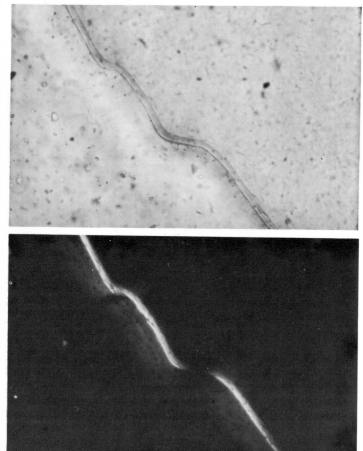

obsidian is visible when a slice of the artefact is examined under an optical microscope at a magnification of × 500. Hydration varies geographically, and several factors such as climate, chemical environment and physical abrasion also affect the thickness of the layer, so that most studies are at present regionally based. Obsidian may also be dated by the fission track dating technique (q.v.).

Ref.: TITE, M. S. *Methods of Physical Examination in Archaeology.* London, 1972, 154–60.

Offset planning

A technique used for planning features and finds on archaeological sites. It is really only suitable for use on sites where small excavation areas are open, and it requires the use of T-squares or simple trigonometry to approach the accuracy of triangulation (q.v.). The method involves the measuring of a point (an object, or the edge of a feature) with reference to a measured baseline, which is frequently the edge of an excavation trench with a tape laid along it. The accurate measurement of distance along the tape and distance from it to the point being planned naturally requires the formation of a right-angle at the point at which the tapes meet. This can be achieved by using a T-square, or by constructing a right-angled triangle with a tape using the Pythagoras theorem (an easy way is to construct a triangle with sides of 3, 4 and 5 units—the side of five units will automatically be opposite a right-angle). Repeating this procedure for every measurement is extremely time-consuming, and since any short cuts taken with the technique tend to lead to inaccuracy, it is better not used on large-scale excavations.

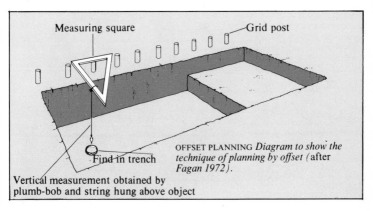

OFFSET PLANNING *Diagram to show the technique of planning by offset (after Fagan 1972).*

Open mould

This is the simplest mould for casting metal; it consists of a single block of stone, or occasionally clay, with the shape of the required artefact cut into it. Only very simple objects can be cast in this way, especially when one surface must be flat; but the moulds continued in use after more sophisticated versions had been developed, mainly for the manufacture of blanks for coins. The moulds were probably not technically open, since this would result in oxidation of the surface of the metal, so probably a flat stone or other cover was placed over the mould during cooling.

Optical emission spectrometry

A long-established technique for the analysis of trace elements in artefacts, particularly metals, pottery, and obsidian and other glasses, in order to identify sources of the raw materials. It involves the excitation, by means of an electric discharge or a laser beam, of the atoms in the sample,

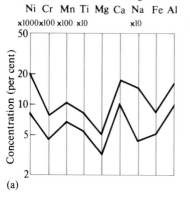

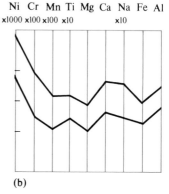

OPTICAL EMISSION SPECTROMETRY
Concentrations of different elements determined by optical emission spectrometry in a. pottery of Mycenaean type from the Peloponnese and, b. pottery of Minoan type from Knossos, Crete, suggesting different clay sources (after Catling and Millett 1965). A stirrup jar from Thebes, Greece, of the type analysed in the study; trace elements in the clay suggest manufacture at or near Khania, Crete.

and the analysis of the constituent wavelengths of the light released when excitation ceases. The wavelengths, separated by the use of a prism or diffraction grating, are each characteristic of individual elements, and the intensity of the light of particular wavelengths indicates the concentration of each element. The typical 10mg. sample is normally dissolved in acid, but recent work has aimed at making the method almost completely non-destructive by the use of a laser beam which vapourizes a few micrograms of material.

Ref.: TITE, M. S. *Methods of Physical Examination in Archaeology.* London, 1972.

Otolith

The name given to the ear-stone of a fish. Otoliths are species-distinctive, and can therefore be used for identification purposes in the analysis of fish

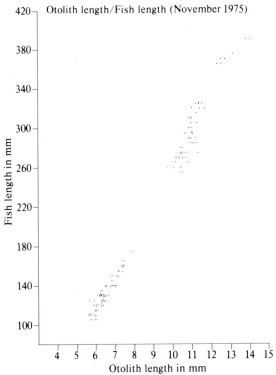

A scatter diagram showing the relationship between OTOLITH *length and total body length in saithe caught in 1975. The two groups represent fish of the first- and second-year age groups (after Mellars 1978). Overleaf Otoliths of saithe from Cnoc Coig Mesolithic shell middens, Oronsay: those on the left are from fish of the second-year age group, those on the right from fish of the first-year age group.*

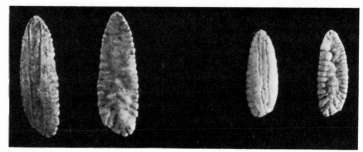

remains from a site. They have an added feature of interest, which is that they grow in annual rings and can thus be used to age the fish and to indicate seasonal use of the site (fishbone analysis, q.v.).

Oxidizing atmosphere

This term, used in pottery technology, describes certain firing conditions which produce particular results. If a kiln is being fired with good, dry fuel and with plenty of draught, the carbon in the fuel is converted into carbon dioxide, and there is oxygen in the atmosphere. This is the oxidizing atmosphere which causes pottery to be fired to a red or orange colour whether it has a slip or not. The opposite phenomenon, a reducing atmosphere (q.v.), produces black pottery; however, much pottery varies in colour over its surface caused by changing conditions during the firing process.

Oxygen isotope analysis

The basis for this technique is the fact that the ratio of two of the stable isotopes of oxygen varies according to the material in which it is found. The oxygen is released from the sample, and is converted to carbon dioxide; the oxygen isotopic ratio is determined after ionization in a mass spectrometer. Glass contains 40–50% oxygen, and therefore the variations in the isotopic ratios for the raw materials can lead to a classification of glass types and even, in some cases, the suggestion of a source for the raw materials. The technique is also used to analyse mollusc shells in an attempt to reconstruct the original aquatic environment of the shell, and hence the source of imported shells, as well as possibly the time of year of their collection. Carbon dioxide is released from the sample of shell, and the isotopic ratios of both the carbon and the oxygen are measured; different water sources produce different ratios. Since shellfish have growth layers like trees, it is possible to analyse the individual outer

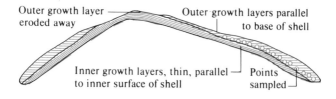

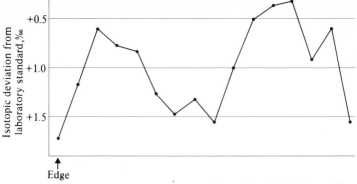

OXYGEN ISOTOPE ANALYSIS Opposite, below *Shell of* patella tabularis *showing the points sampled for isotopic analysis (*after Shackleton 1973*). Isotopic analyses from the shell show the range in isotopic composition which, when compared with water temperatures during the same period, allows the estimation of sea temperature, suggesting in turn the season of collection of that shell (*after Shackleton 1973*).*

layer and to show by the isotopic data, which can be affected by seasonal variation, the actual season of collection.

Ref.: SHACKLETON, N. J. 'Stable isotope study of the palaeoenvironment of the Neolithic site of Nea Nikomedia, Greece', *Nature* 227 (1979), 943–4.

Palaeobotany

The study of plant remains from the past. It includes material which has no direct connection with man and his activities, and is thus less specific to archaeology than palaeoethnobotany (q.v.) or archaeobotany (q.v.); however, these terms continue to be used interchangeably.

Palaeoethnobotany

The study of the plant remains associated with man's past. It concentrates on those which he gathered and those which he grew deliberately, found in archaeological contexts. The study of plant remains has been made possible since the development of analytical techniques such as pollen analysis (q.v.), and new recovery techniques like flotation (q.v.). The extraction of pollen grains from suitable archaeological deposits has been carried out for many years, but the flotation of large numbers of samples to yield macroscopic plant remains is a relatively new procedure. There is now a much larger body of material with which to work. The earliest stages of man's interaction with his environment comprised the gathering of wild flora—fruit and berries, grasses and roots—the remains of which can be occasionally found among occupational debris on a cave or camp site; they can also be retrieved by the study of coprolites (q.v.). It is, however, with the beginnings of farming that there is a great increase in the available data, since there is more agricultural activity on the settlement site, and the chance of locating stores of seed grain.

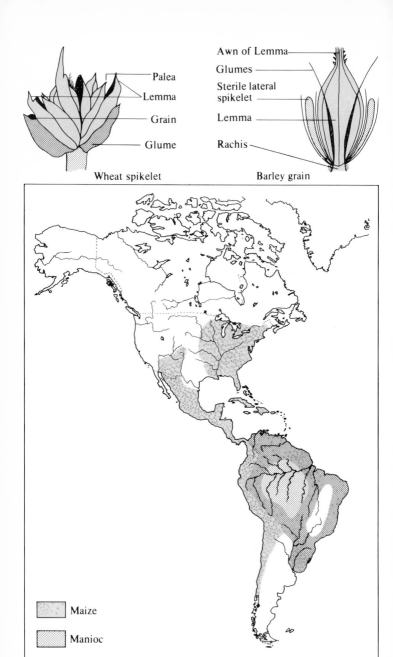

Palea
Lemma
Grain
Glume

Wheat spikelet

Awn of Lemma
Glumes
Sterile lateral
spikelet
Lemma
Rachis

Barley grain

Maize

Manioc

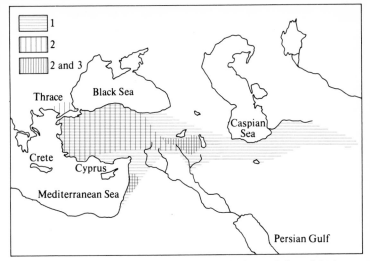

PALAEOETHNOBOTANY Opposite, above *Diagram of Wheat spikelet and Barley grain.* Opposite, below *Distribution of maize and manioc in the Americas (after Wissler 1957).* Above *Distribution of the wild progenitors of cultivated crops, showing the areas where agriculture began (after Piggott 1965).*

The onset of farming is a particularly interesting area of study for the palaeoethnobotanist, since the development of cultivated crops from their wild ancestors has not yet been fully understood, especially as it is not easy to distinguish wild grasses from the earliest cultivated ones. The areas where farming began are those where suitable varieties of wild grasses and other crops had their habitat. Cultivation of crops did not start everywhere at the same time, however, and wheat and barley were grown in Asia some time before maize and manioc in the Americas. The interest of the palaeoethnobotanist is not just in the beginning of farming: the introduction of new crops, such as oats, rye, rice, millet, beans and potatoes implies diversification and the adaptation of plants to different climatic conditions. The reconstruction of the total diet, as well as the use of vegetational materials for other purposes such as thatching or basketry, are other areas of study in this field.

Ref.: RENFREW, J. M. *Palaeoethnobotany.* London, 1973.

Palaeointensity dating *see* MAGNETIC DATING

Palaeontology

This is the term given to the study of all fossil organisms. It is concerned with flora and fauna, and, as human palaeontology, with the origins of man.

Palaeopathology

The study of disease in antiquity, both animal and human, though the term tends to be identified with the latter. By the study of the health of a

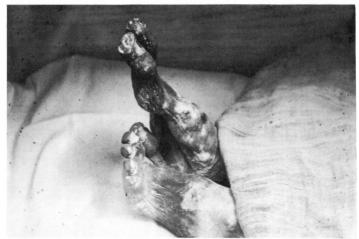

PALAEOPATHOLOGY *The club foot of Pharaoh Siptah, XXth Dynasty, Egypt.*

group much may be learnt of life expectancy and population statistics, while general good or bad health may be a contributory reason for the success or failure of a particular population. Most of the material studied is osteological, though soft tissue may be analysed when preserved, as in the case of mummification or bog preservation. Congenital malformations may show relationships between skeletons; diseases such as arthritis, tuberculosis, syphilis and leprosy can be identified, as well as such conditions as bone fracture through injury.

Palaeopedology

The study of fossil soils, which includes material in both geological and archaeological contexts. Soil scientists can assist archaeologists by explaining the natural and man-influenced processes on archaeological sites, such as the manner of filling of certain types of feature. Information of potentially greater interest can be deduced from some deposits, such as climatic and environmental variation, which can lead to conclusions about the manipulation of the landscape by man.

Ref.: CORNWALL, I. W. *Soils for the Archaeologist.* London, 1958.

Palaeoserology

The study of blood and blood groups in antiquity. Results have been obtained from mummified and frozen bodies, and research concentrates on family groupings among mummified remains, though also diseases can be studied (palaeopathology, q.v.) through the examination of blood.

Ref.: LENGYEL, I. A. *Palaeoserology: blood-typing with the fluorescent antibody method.* Budapest, 1975.

Palynology *see* POLLEN ANALYSIS

Particle size analysis

This is a technique for analysing the grain sizes of archaeological or geological sediments (q.v.) with the aim of understanding the manner and process of their deposition. The technique also allows the accurate description of a deposit, and comparison with other sediments in more detailed fashion than simply by words like silt. There are several methods of particle size analysis, and the one used depends partly on the degree of detail required and partly on the nature of the deposit, which may range from pebbles through gravel, sand and silt to clay. Dry sieving, the sifting of deposits through various sizes of mesh so that particles are grouped into sizes, is suitable for larger grains from pebbles to coarse sand, while light or electron microscopy can cope with finer grains of sand, silt and clay. Sedimentation, the counting of grains dispersed in liquid as they fall to the bottom of a container, is suitable for the finest grains of silt and clay. A combination of methods, for example dry sieving and sedimentation, is frequently used. The results are plotted in one of several forms of graph. The analysis may yield information on whether the deposit is wind- or water-borne, how much it has weathered, and to what extent it has been affected by man.

Ref.: SHACKLEY, M. L. *Archaeological Sediments.* London, 1975.

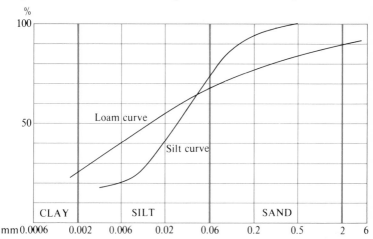

PARTICLE SIZE ANALYSIS *Graphs of particle size of deposits from Cassington (loam), and Stanton Harcourt (silt), Oxfordshire, England, showing the difference between the curves (*after *Cornwall 1953).*

Patina

This is the outer surface layer of an artefact which may differ in colour, texture and substance from the inner part of the object because of physical or chemical alteration due to the environment in which it has lain. Thus flint often has a white or bluish patina obscuring its natural darker colour, though this may become stained with brown or yellow due to contacts with iron compounds in percolating water. Similarly, the green patina on bronze objects is a product of chemical change, and is, in essence, a form of corrosion.

Pattern burnishing *see* BURNISH

Pattern welding
A technique of ironworking used particularly in the manufacture of weapons, developed in an attempt to overcome the problems of brittleness caused by trying to diffuse carbon into iron. Though the pattern is a by-product and not the aim of the technique, the distinctive visual aspect doubtless showed the blade's quality. In the manufacture of a sword, for example, the central part would typically be a core of carbon steel, with soft iron welded to it. Twisted carburized strips were welded to each side, and then cutting edges of medium carburized steel were welded to the edges. The pattern derives from the difference in the carbon content between the uncarburized cores and the carburized surfaces of the welded strips, which is exposed during the forging and grinding of the weapon. It is estimated that a sword of this quality could have taken some 75 hours to make.

Ref.: MARYON, H. 'Pattern-welding and damascening of sword blades', *Studies in Conservation* 5 (1960), 25–37.

Petrological microscopy
The petrological microscope is used in the examination of thin-sections of stone artefacts or pottery (ceramic petrology, q.v.), in order to identify, and eventually locate, the geographical source of the rocks or minerals present. A slice, approximately 1mm. thick, is removed from the artefact, and is ground down until completely smooth; it is then stuck to a glass microscope slide, and the other side is then ground down to produce an almost transparent slice which can then be examined under the micros-cope. The petrological microscope has a polarizer and an analyser which

PETROLOGICAL MICROSCOPY *A thin section of porphyritic andesite from California, photographed in plane-polarised light.*

transmits the light vibrating in one direction only; the reaction of various minerals to this type of light allows their identification by several different methods. If then a comparison is made with putative source materials it may be possible to identify the source of the raw material from which the artefact has been made.

Ref.: HARTSHORNE, N. H. and STUART, A. *Crystals and the Polarising Microscope.* 4th ed. London, 1970.

pH analysis

A technique used for measuring the pH, or acidity or alkalinity of a soil. The results of the test will show the measure of pH, and will thus suggest what type of remains are to be expected. In an acid soil bones will not survive, but pollen grains will; in an alkaline soil there will be only rare occurrences of pollen, but bones should be more plentiful. The pH is tested by moistening a sample of soil with neutral distilled water and dipping into it a pre-prepared indicator paper; the resulting colour, which depends on the pH content, can be matched against prepared charts of known pH values.

Phosphate analysis

A technique for detecting the presence of phosphate in soil. A concentration of phosphate indicates the former presence of bone in acid soils where it is easily destroyed, and also, since it derives from body wastes, areas of concentrated occupation by humans or animals. The analysis of soils for archaeological purposes can thus pinpoint settlement areas, as well as burials totally decayed. The technique can be applied in a variety of ways, but normally an extract of the soil is made in hydrochloric acid; the liquid is added to ammonium molybdate solution, and the occurrence of a heavy yellow precipitate indicates the presence of phosphate. The test is very sensitive, and insignificant amounts of phosphate will still produce a yellow precipitate.

Photogrammetry

A technique for the mapping of areas using photographs taken directly from above. Though used mainly in map-making, it can also be used for the planning of archaeological sites. For large-scale map-making the photographs are taken from the air, a sequence along each flight path with each exposure overlapping the next by 60%. Adjustment is made so that the photographs can be laid side by side in a mosaic, with common reference points lying over each other. They are then converted into maps by the use of multiple projectors. A similar technique can be used to plan smaller-scale features such as excavations. The camera can be mounted on a rigid frame, and moved along so that it takes overlapping vertical photographs. The method is particularly useful where a large area of stone or rubble needs to be planned in detail but, because of rescue situations, the time cannot be allowed while the site is open; drawing can therefore be carried out at a later stage when the excavation has finished.

Photomicrograph

A photograph of an object or part of an object taken at high magnification

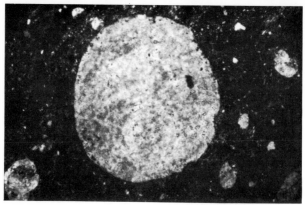

A PHOTOMICROGRAPH *of ooliths in the fabric of an Iron Age pot from Danebury, Hampshire, England; their presence suggests the Jurassic ridge as a source for the temper in the clay. Mag. × 18.*

in order to reveal details of form and structure. Many of these are taken automatically for record purposes during the use of such instruments as the scanning electron microscope (q.v.), the petrological microscope (q.v.) and the optical microscope. Photomicrographs can reveal the detailed structure of pollen grains for identification purposes, the presence of different tempering materials in pottery, or the details of grain structure in metals which can help to identify metalworking procedures.

Phytolith

This is a silica body found within the cells of certain plants, especially grasses and cereals, which may be located in archaeological deposits where other parts of the plant have disintegrated. The presence of these microscopic bodies may help to reconstruct the original flora of a site, though not all phytolith types appear to be species-diagnostic. The well-known phenomenon of sickle gloss (q.v.) is caused by the wear of the sickle blade on these silica bodies.

Pie chart

A form of visual representation of quantitative data, which involves drawing a circle representative of the total of units, and marking off segments like slices in the proportions of the percentages of different categories present. This sort of chart is less suitable than the bar chart (q.v.) when either there are categories with no entries from a particular assemblage, or when there are too many categories for ease of representation.

Pisé

A building material, mud or clay, which is not preformed into separate bricks, but which is shaped into walls *in situ*. The clay dries hard in the sun but the resulting walls would not survive heavy rainfall.

Plane-table

A piece of equipment much used in earlier surveying and map-making.

Other methods such as photogrammetry (q.v.) have now taken its place, since they are less laborious and more accurate, but there are still occasions where its use is warranted. It is a drawing-board used in conjunction with an alidade (q.v.), set on a tripod and levelled by the spirit level on the alidade. One end of the alidade is held on the point on the map representing the point of operation, and the other is directed at a marker on the point to be plotted. This gives the angle from the point of operation, and distance can be plotted directly along the ruler after scaling down from the original measurement.

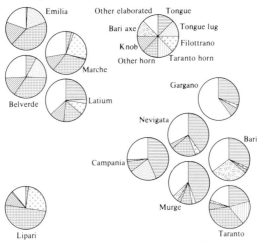

Regional differences in the relative frequency of handle types on Italian Appenine culture pottery presented in the form of PIE CHARTS *(after Trump 1958).*

Plantago

One of the weeds of cultivation (q.v.), which appear strongly in the pollen record as a result of the clearing of previously wooded land. There are several varieties, for example *Plantago lanceolata, Plantago major,* and their presence is taken by archaeologists to imply cereal cultivation.

Ploughwash

A sediment of slopewash (q.v.) type caused by man's farming activities in breaking up the soil on hills or slopes. The cultivation of soil for crops, or the intensive pasturing of animals, causes a change in the structure of the soil which may result in poor drainage; combined with the lack of vegetation, this causes the soil to move downhill.

Point of percussion

A term associated with the manufacture of flint tools; it describes the point at which the core is struck with a hammerstone in order to remove a flake. The point of percussion is a visible excrescence on the core, a small scar on the struck flake; the bulb of percussion (q.v.) surrounds it.

Pollen analysis

This technique, which is used in establishing relative chronologies as well as in environmental archaeology, has been practised for many years. Developed primarily as a technique for the relative dating of natural horizons, it is used more and more as a monitor of changes in the environment of man, both naturally and anthropogenically induced. The pollen grains of trees, shrubs, grasses and flowers are preserved in either anaerobic (q.v.) conditions or in acid soils, since the outer layer of the grain is very resilient. Samples can be taken from the deposits by means of a core, for example from a peat bog, or from individual layers at frequent intervals in a section face on an archaeological site. Pollen is extracted from the sample by various means such as destroying the soil around it with acid. The pollen is then concentrated and stained for greater clarity, and examined under a microscope. Pollen grains are identifiable by their shape, and the percentages of the different species present in each sample are recorded on a pollen diagram. A comparison of the pollen diagrams for different levels within a deposit allows the identification of changes in the percentages of species and thus changes in the environment.

As a dating technique, pollen has been used to identify different zones of arboreal vegetation which are judged to correspond to climatic changes: an object or site which can be associated with a layer of peat could be dated by the pollen zone to a climatic horizon (for example, an interglacial). Once radiocarbon dating was developed this use of pollen analysis became less important. However, it became apparent with further study of less major elements in the pollen diagram that appearances and disappearances of certain species could be linked with local variations in land use. The elm decline (q.v.) and landnam (q.v.) could be clearly seen, as well as the presence of weeds of cultivation (q.v.) which

POLLEN ANALYSIS: *A pollen diagram for Nant Ffrancon, Wales, lake sediments, showing presence/absence of tree and shrub pollens and the ratio (AP = arboreal pollen, NAP = non-arboreal pollen) between the two at different periods (after Seddon 1962).*

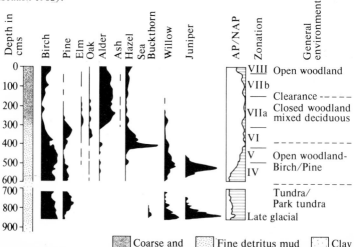

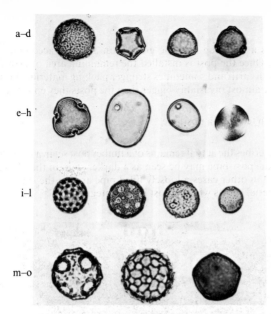

Photomicrographs of pollen grains. a. *elm;* b. *alder;* c. *hazel;* d. *birch;* e. *lime;* f. *rye;* g. *wave hairgrass;* h. *field maple;* i. *fat hen;* j. *ragged robin;* k. *ribwort plantain;* l. *sheep's bit;* m. *common fumitory;* n. *persicalia;* o. *hornbeam.*

could point to agriculture even when cereal grains or pollen were not recovered. There are still certain problems which must always be borne in mind, such as the occasional tendency for pollen to move down through the soil into earlier levels, and the fact that certain pollens such as tree pollens travel further than herbaceous pollens and thus reflect regional rather than local conditions. Despite this the technique has still an enormous amount to reveal about man's natural and man-influenced environment.

Ref.: DIMBLEBY, G. W. *Plants and Archaeology.* 2nd ed. London, 1978.

Port of trade

A town or city whose specific function is to act as a meeting place for foreign traders. Though most frequently located on coasts or rivers, this is not necessary, and such sites could equally be inland at the junction of different geographical regions. The residents do not themselves engage in trading expeditions, but serve as a centre for transshipment and storage of goods; the site is characterized by facilities for storage. Trade is administered by the local political authorities, and such sites are most commonly small political units, independent of larger neighbouring groups who receive supplies through them. Ports of trade are known from many different parts of the world, such as Tyre and Sidon, and may have been one of the most important modes of early long-distance trade.

Posthole

A posthole is a hole dug into the ground on a site to accommodate a timber post. Once the post is installed the remaining area of posthole is backfilled with earth and sometimes stronger packing material like stone. Postholes are almost invariably bigger than the posts they contained.

Post-mould

The American term for a posthole.

Post-pipe

This term describes the actual remains of a timber post set in a posthole. In some cases the post-pipe may be seen as a darker stain in the centre of a posthole, but in other cases a loosely filled pipe area in the surrounding packing material shows where a post has disintegrated.

A section of the chalk-cut palisade trench at Rams Hill, Berkshire, England, showing the POST PIPE *(darker area). The scale represents 30 cm.*

Potassium-argon dating

A chronometric dating technique which is based on the decay of a radioactive material into a non-radioactive material at a known rate. Potassium, which is present in most rocks and minerals, has a single radioactive isotope, K 40. This decays by two different processes into Calcium 40 and Argon 40. Though 89% decays to Calcium 40, it is not suitable for measurement since most rocks contain Calcium 40 as a primary element, and the amount caused by the decay of K 40 cannot be determined. The remaining 11% decays into the gas Argon 40, and this can be measured, along with the amount of potassium in the sample, to give a date. There are various sources of error in the method, such as contamination by atmospheric argon; the effect of this is worse the younger the material, so that the technique is used on material more than 100,000 years old. The method is used generally on volcanic rock, since the melting associated with its formation removes almost all pre-existing Argon 40. In order to date an archaeological deposit, therefore, it should link up in some way with a volcanic layer like pumice. Samples are normally collected by a specialist. The rock is melted, driving off Argon 40 as a gas whose ratio to other argon isotopes produced by irradiation is determined in a mass spectrometer. Dates produced by using this technique have been checked by fission track dating (q.v.), which is not subject to the same sources of possible errors. The technique has been used most successfully in the dating of layers associated with the earliest remains of hominids, particularly in Africa.

Ref.: DALRYMPLE, G. and LANPHERE, M. A. *Potassium-argon dating.* San Francisco, 1969.

Potin
A bronze alloy with a high tin content, between standard bronze and speculum (q.v.). It was used particularly, and the term is normally employed, for a type of coinage current in western Europe in the first centuries BC and AD; the tin content varied between 7% and 27%.

Pressure flaking
A method for the secondary working (q.v.) of flint tools which can be achieved using various techniques. The roughed-out form of the tool is

PRESSURE FLAKING *by resting the tool on a piece of leather and applying pressure with a bone point.* Below *Knife, pre-Dynastic (before 3,100 BC) from Gebel Arak, Egypt, showing pressure-flaked blade. Length 25.3 cm.*

sharpened and finished by exerting pressure with a bone or a stick on the edge in order to remove small thin chips. This produces an extremely sharp edge on the tool which, should it become blunt after much use, can be sharpened by removing a few more flakes. Fine-edged weapons, such as daggers, can be produced using this technique.

Primary silt

This term defines the material which collects in the bottom of a newly dug feature (ditch, gully, pit, etc.) as a result of the immediate weathering of the sides and top due to wind or the action of precipitation. Unless the feature was cleaned of this material in antiquity, it may be recognized in many archaeological features, and any material found in it may date from around the time of the original digging. However, older artefacts lying around on the original ground surface may have been blown or kicked in during the primary silting, so finds from this context could be older than the feature itself.

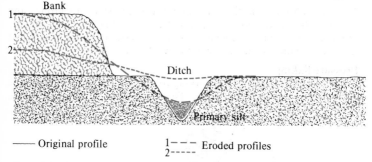

—— Original profile   1 – – –   Eroded profiles
                            2 -----

Diagrammatic section of an earthwork and ditch showing PRIMARY SILTING *and final filling of ditch.*

Processual archaeology

A branch of archaeology which seeks to understand the nature of culture change by a study of the variables which bring it about. The approach to explanation adheres to that followed in the natural sciences: after observation, questions are formulated, hypotheses are formed to answer the questions and are tested against the data. The ultimate aim is the formulation of laws.

Ref.: BINFORD, L. R. 'Archaeological systematics and the study of cultural process', *American Antiquity* 31 (1965), 203–10.

Proton gradiometer

An instrument used in magnetic surveying (q.v.) for detecting the presence of magnetic anomalies. This instrument is simpler, slightly less sensitive and considerably cheaper than the absolute proton magnetometer (q.v.). There are two detector bottles filled with water or alcohol placed at either end of a staff two metres long and held vertically during operation. Protons which form the nuclei of hydrogen atoms in the liquid gyrate or precess (*see* proton magnetometer); the frequency of precession is identical in the two bottles if no anomaly is present. Any disturbance in the magnetic intensity caused, for example, by a buried feature, results in a different frequency in the two bottles. The signals therefore get out of step, and a significant beat is observed which may be read off a meter or, in the case of a 'bleeper', may be heard through an earphone or loudspeaker.

Ref.: AITKEN, M. J. and TITE, M. S., 'A gradient magnetometer, using proton free-precession', *Journ. Scient. Instr.* 39 (1962), 625–9.

Proton magnetometer

One of the instruments used in magnetic surveying (q.v.) for detecting changes in magnetic field intensity. The sensitivity achieved by the complex electrical circuits makes it one of the most popular instruments, but its very complexity makes it more expensive than other forms of equipment. The detector consists of a bottle of alcohol or water round which is wound an electrical coil of 1,000 turns. The protons, which form the nuclei of hydrogen atoms in the liquid, spin like tops, gyrating in their attempt to align themselves in the direction of the earth's magnetic field; these gyrations vary in direct proportion to the magnetic field intensity. A current of one amp is passed through the coil for three seconds, which aligns the majority of the protons in the direction of the magnetic field thus produced. When this current is cut off the protons attempt to realign in the direction of the earth's magnetic field; the speed of gyration, or frequency of precession, is amplified and measured in the instrument and reflects any alteration in the magnetic intensity caused by the presence of fired structures, soil disturbances (e.g. pits, ditches, etc.) or iron objects. The measurements are displayed on the instrument, and are read off by the operator at the instrument end. The person holding the bottle, which is attached to the instrument by a long cable, moves along a pre-set grid over the site, and readings are made at suitable and constant intervals.

Ref.: WATERS, G. S. and FRANCIS, P. D., 'A nuclear magnetometer', *Journ. Scient. Instr.* 35 (1958), 88–93.

Prototype

This term can have two slightly different meanings. In one sense a prototype is the first in a series of artefacts, the earliest form of some type which later develops—for example, the first of a new type of pottery. In another sense a prototype is a model after which objects are copied: the prototype for a clay wine jar could be a metal wine jug of similar shape, made in the same region or at least seen by the potter.

Proximal

The part of a long bone (arm or leg) which is nearest the body. The opposite end is the distal.

Pulsed induction meter

An instrument used in electromagnetic surveying (q.v.). It is used mainly for the detection of metals, though on a limited scale it can be used to locate archaeological features. The instrument has a transmitter coil, which sends pulses of magnetic field to the ground: the continuous rising and falling of the field produces eddy currents in metal objects, and magnetic fields in susceptible soil. These are detected by a receiver coil. Only shallow features can be satisfactorily located, so that the instrument is better used as a detector of metals.

Ref.: COLANI, C. 'A new type of locating device. I. The Instrument', *Archaeometry* 9 (1966), 3–8.

Quadrant method

A technique developed for the excavation of circular and subcircular upstanding features, used most widely in the examination of burial mounds or barrows. Before the complete removal of the feature, it allows a look at all four quarters, at two complete cross-sections, and at part of the centre. Material is extracted from four quarters of the feature, starting with the two opposite each other and ending with the other two. The quadrants are slightly offset, so that the outer face of the west baulk of one is continuous (in reverse) with the outer face of the east baulk of its opposite, this continuous section going through the centre of the feature. After the recording of the sections, the baulks may be removed and the remainder of the centre excavated. Although mainly used for burial mounds, the technique is suitable for the excavation of pits where it is considered useful to examine tiplines in two directions.

Excavation of a barrow (burial mound) at West Heath, Sussex, by the QUADRANT METHOD, *showing the baulks still standing.*

Quenching

A procedure in metalworking involving the rapid cooling of a red-hot metal by plunging it into cold water. The resulting metalwork is softer than when allowed to cool slowly. The difference is insignificant in copper or bronze working, but for iron and steel quenching produces a different structure, much harder and more brittle. Quenched steel can be made less brittle by heating gently. Steel can be tempered by reheating until the required colour appears (tempering, q.v.) and immediately quenching.

Radiocarbon dating

One of the best-known chronometric dating techniques (q.v.), which can be used for the dating of most organic material up to 70,000 years old. It is based on the theory propounded by W. Libby in 1949 that cosmic rays bombarding the earth's atmosphere produce neutrons, which interact with nitrogen (N14) to produce the radioactive carbon isotope C14. In the form of carbon dioxide C14 enters plants by photosynthesis, and thus is taken into the food chain by animals who eat the plants. This process of incorporation of C14 continues until the organism dies, and at that point the radioactive isotope C14 begins to decay into non-radioactive N14. The half-life (q.v.) of radiocarbon is known: assuming that the C12/C14 ratio has remained constant through time, it should be possible to measure the remaining C14 in a sample and thus determine its age.

One of the basic assumptions of the technique is that the amount of

RADIOCARBON DATING *The combustion/purification train in a radiocarbon dating laboratory.*

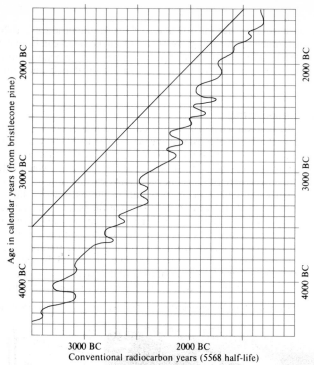

2000 BC

3000 BC

4000 BC

Age in calendar years (from bristlecone pine)

2000 BC

3000 BC

4000 BC

3000 BC   2000 BC

Conventional radiocarbon years (5568 half-life)

A calibration chart for radiocarbon dates, showing the gradually diverging lines of radiocarbon years and calendar years as calculated from dendrochronology. The wiggly bristlecone pine curve is undergoing revision, and can only be considered as an approximation (after Renfrew 1973).

radiocarbon in the atmosphere has remained constant through time. It is clear now, with the establishment of a dendrochronological sequence for the bristlecone pine (q.v.), that the C14 concentration has fluctuated, since radiocarbon dates have been too young for the calendrical sequence; the reasons for the fluctuation are not yet fully understood. The calibration (q.v.) of radiocarbon dates is therefore necessary in order to achieve an approximate date in calendar years. Dates quoted in radiocarbon years, before calibration, are written b.c. or b.p. (before present), as opposed to calibrated dates, written B.C. or B.P. The original half-life for radiocarbon of 5,568 ± 30 years has been revised to 5,730 ± 40 years, though dates are normally published according to the old half-life in order to avoid confusion (the date can be adjusted for the new half-life by multiplying the old date by 1.029). All radiocarbon dates are quoted with a standard deviation (q.v.), and since this only represents a 66% certainty that the date lies within the range quoted, the dates should never be used without the error stated. Ideally a series of dates should be obtained for any one deposit, since a single date can be subject to error caused by a number of factors, and a series may cluster around a central point, allowing more confidence to be attached to the date.

New refinements are constantly being added to the technique which improve its accuracy as well as extend the range of dates which can be achieved. A previous limit of 50,000 years on the age of material which could be dated, set by the limits on the ability of the proportional counter used to record beta particle emissions, has been extended to 70,000 years by the use of isotopic enrichment, the artificial enrichment of the $C14$ to $C12$ ratio. The procedures for collecting, cleaning and decontaminating samples before the chemical preparation for dating have also been improved. Theoretically, all organic materials can be dated by the method, from charcoal and bone to shell and cloth, but in practice results are better with some substances than others. Though there are doubtless more adjustments and improvements to come, the technique has already been vindicated by the revolutionary effects it has had on world prehistory.

Ref.: OLSSON, I. U. ed. *Radiocarbon Variations and Absolute Chronology.* New York, 1970.

Radiography

This technique involves the application of high-energy electromagnetic radiation to specimens in order to study details of structure, decoration or composition invisible to the naked eye. X-rays are normally used, though gamma-rays may be employed in circumstances where an X-ray tube is difficult to manipulate. The object is placed on photographic film and is subjected to X-rays; differential absorption of the rays denotes variations in composition, and these are shown on the film as contrasting light and dark areas. This form of examination has been used particularly on iron objects where rust and corrosion products prevent proper study of the object: non-ferrous metal inlays, for example silver, can be revealed since they absorb more X-rays. Radiography is also used in the study of biological material, for example bone and especially mummies, and microradiographic techniques have been developed (X-ray microscopy) for both biological and metallographic examination.

Ref.: TITE, M. S. *Methods of Physical Examination in Archaeology.* London, 1972, 252–4.

Radiometric assay *see* URANIUM TEST

Raised beach

A raised, or fossil, beach is a geological feature produced by changing sea-levels through time. Though it may now be some distance from the sea, a raised beach shows where the original coastline was, and also makes it clear that searching for contemporary archaeological sites between it and the present shoreline is unnecessary since that area would have been submerged.

The RAISED BEACH *platform near Lannacombe, Devon, England.*

Rank

The position held by an individual on the basis of his status within a society where statuses are not all equal, but are graded into a hierarchical structure. A society with such inequalities of status is called a ranked society.

Rank-size rule

A general relationship between the size of a settlement and its rank within

The RANK-SIZE RULE *applied to Welsh hillforts of the first millennium* BC. *The predicted pattern is shown by the straight line. The rule does not work perfectly for very small sites, and the largest are not as big as expected, showing that the settlement pattern is not fully developed, nor dominated by a single major site (after Hodder 1977).*

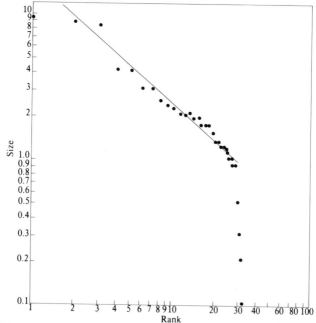

a set of settlements, first suggested by the German geographer F. Auerbach. If sites are ranked in order of size (1st, 2nd, 3rd, . . .), the population of the *n*th will be 1/*n* the size of the largest; thus the 3rd site will be ⅓ the size of the largest. The rule works best in areas of complex economic and political organization, with comparatively long histories of urban development; on the other hand, areas with simpler organization and shorter periods of urbanization are often dominated by one or more very large sites. There is also apparently a minimum size of site below which the rule does not fit the data. It has been suggested that this relationship represents a natural balance of settlement growth. There are problems in its application to archaeological examples, especially the estimation of the size of settlements, but it has been shown that Roman walled towns fit the rule well.

Ref.: HODDER, I. and ORTON, C. *Spatial Analysis in Archaeology.* London, 1976, 69–73.

Reciprocity
A form of primitive exchange in which goods are transferred between individuals or groups of the same status without any central control, usually in a balanced and mutually beneficial manner; the exchange can frequently be regarded as an expression of the social obligations between the parties. In a small social group such as a family, generalized reciprocity occurs, in which the emphasis is on giving, with no expectation of immediate return. Within a wider social circle, for instance between families in the same community, balanced reciprocity takes place, where both parties expect to give and receive goods to approximately the same value; though there is no fixed price or standard of value, all parties have an idea of the worth of what they give. With people still further removed, such as strangers from another community, negative reciprocity may be practised, whereby both sides attempt to receive more than they give; the extreme case of this is raiding, where the transfer of goods is in one direction only. The items exchanged in such reciprocal economies may be utilitarian goods, foodstuffs or prestige materials. Societies which practise redistribution (q.v.) for their internal exchange may well have a relationship of reciprocity with neighbours. (*See also* EXCHANGE).

Redistribution
A form of primitive exchange in which the flow of goods is directed to and from, and controlled by, a central authority. It might involve the physical collection and pooling of locally produced items and their subsequent reallocation, or merely control of the flow without central collection. Storage capacity and a system of record-keeping are often associated with the central power. The goods exchanged in such a system may be local products, in which case the control of allocation may permit some degree of craft specialization, since the specialists will be able to depend on the central authority for the supply of all necessities; some part of the local products may be retained for exchange with external communities. The

exotic products received in return for these exports may be treated as items of prestige, and made available to only a restricted number of the local people in the upper levels of the social hierarchy (q.v.). Redistribution presupposes the existence of a central power, and is often associated with societies organized as chiefdoms (q.v.) with a central authority and marked differences in social ranking. (*See also* EXCHANGE).

Reducing atmosphere
This term describes particular pottery firing conditions where the supply of air is limited or the fuel damp. The fuel does not totally burn under these circumstances, and the gases contain carbon monoxide rather than oxygen. This generally results in black-surfaced pottery as opposed to the red produced in an oxidizing atmosphere (q.v.), though shades of colour may vary on a single pot if conditions during firing are not stable.

Relative dating
Techniques of dating where phases or objects can be put into a sequence relative to each other, but which are not tied into calendrically measured time. Before the advent of chronometric (q.v.) dating techniques, all dating was relative except where links with historical events could be proved. Some of these techniques are still useful where chronometric dates cannot be obtained. Chief among them are stratigraphy (q.v.) and seriation (q.v.), as well as those scientific techniques like fluorine tests (q.v.) on bone. Theoretically, floating chronologies (q.v.) which cannot be tied down to an absolute date (for example, certain dendrochronological sequences) are relative chronologies, even though the techniques are essentially chronometric.

Repoussé
A technique for the decoration of metal objects, usually carried out on bronze, though also used on gold and silver. It consists of hammering up the design from the back of the object using round-edged punches. The surface of the raised design can then be decorated, usually by accentuating the hammered design with chasing (q.v.). This technique of decoration can only be carried out on thin metal sheeting.

Rescue archaeology
Threats to archaeological remains and to whole areas of the landscape have increased greatly in the last two decades. These threats occur in the form of road-building, road improvement, new building of houses, offices and industrial complexes, the flooding of valleys for reservoirs, and improved farming techniques involving the use of deep ploughing. The rescue, or salvage, archaeologist, is concerned with the retrieval of as much information as possible about the archaeological sites before they are damaged or destroyed. Frequently time is too short and funds too limited for anything but a watching brief to be attempted. Though the term usually implies excavation of a site, it is not, and should not be, always necessary. While destruction increases and funds do not, a policy for determining the best use of resources should be formulated, which

would result in more recording, more research-oriented excavation, and less hasty sample trenching. The tendency of rescue archaeology in the 1960s to attempt excavation of every site, however badly, simply because it was threatened, is beginning to give way to a more ordered policy.

Ref.: RAHTZ, P. A. (ed.). *Rescue Archaeology.* Harmondsworth, 1974.

Resistivity surveying

This is a technique used for the location of buried features which compares well with magnetic surveying (q.v.), first because the instruments used are simple and therefore cheap, and secondly because modern features such as power cables, iron scrap and standing buildings do not affect the readings. The relative slowness of operation, however, makes it less convenient to use than a magnetometer, and it is not as efficient for locating isolated features such as pits. It is used mainly for the location and planning before (or instead of) excavation of linear features such as walls or ditches. The technique involves the measurement of the resistance of the earth to an electric current passing between metal electrodes. Dry rocks and soils do not conduct electricity, but the resistivity is lowered when they contain water, and the varying amounts of resistance encountered reflect the different conducting properties of features below the surface. A ditch cut into rock and filled with soil will produce an area of low resistance, while a wall or other stone feature surrounded by soil will register a high resistance. The location of features in this way can be hampered by local geological conditions which may produce changes over a small area with their own differing resistivities; these might be difficult to distinguish from changes caused by archaeological features. Recent rain may also affect the conditions in buried ditches or surrounding topsoil. Instruments have been developed specifically for use in archaeology; electrodes may be placed in a number of different arrays, each with their own advantages and disadvantages, so there are choices in the mode of

The results of RESISTIVITY SURVEY *across a wall with the electrode array broadside or end on to the feature, showing the high resistivity encountered over the stones in contrast to the low resistivity of the surrounding area (*after *Tite 1972).*

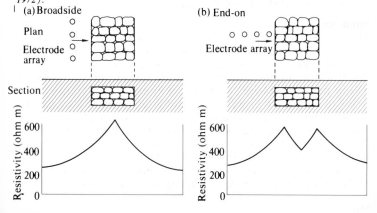

operation. Certainly the best results from this form of location technique come from operators well-skilled in its handling.

Ref.: CLARK, A. 'Resistivity Surveying', in *Science and Archaeology.* ed. D. Brothwell and E. Higgs. 2nd ed. London 1969, 695–707.

Retouch

The work done to a flint implement after its preliminary roughing-out in order to make it into a functional tool. In the case of a core-tool, such as a hand-axe, retouch may simply consist of roughly trimming the edge by striking with a hammerstone, but on smaller, finer flake or blade tools it is usually carried out by pressure-flaking (q.v.). Retouch, also known as secondary working, is one of the most obvious features distinguishing a man-made from a naturally struck flint.

Robber trench

A word used in excavation to describe a feature created by the robbing of its original filling material. In areas where stone or other building materials are scarce, or where a new structure is being built near one which is disused, a monument may be plundered of its building materials. The trenches where the walls once stood and where the stone has been removed are called robber trenches or ghost walls. A good excavator should be able to reconstruct a plan of the original structure from careful examination and recording of the robber trenches.

Rustication

The roughening of the surface of a pot which may or may not have an applied slip (q.v.). The roughening may be achieved using fingers, finger-nails, twigs, etc., and though it may be conceived of as pure decoration, in most cases it is probably a device to prevent a greasy pot slipping through the fingers. In some cases a grit such as flint may actually be added to the roughened clay to give additional grip.

Salvage archaeology

The American term for rescue archaeology, q.v.

Sampling

The process of selecting part of the evidence from a field of study as a basis for generalizing about the whole. In a loose sense, all archaeological field-work and excavation is sampling, since it is impossible to collect all the data from the complex mass of an archaeological site. The parts selected may be purely haphazard, being dictated by expediency, availability or threat of destruction (sometimes termed a 'grab sample'), or may be determined by the need for particular evidence for a specific question (a 'judgement sample'); the question itself will be determined by the existing framework of archaeological thought. In neither case can the sample be used as a reliable basis for estimating the whole.

In a more specific sense, sampling, or more fully probabilistic or random sampling, uses the theory of probability to make estimates of how

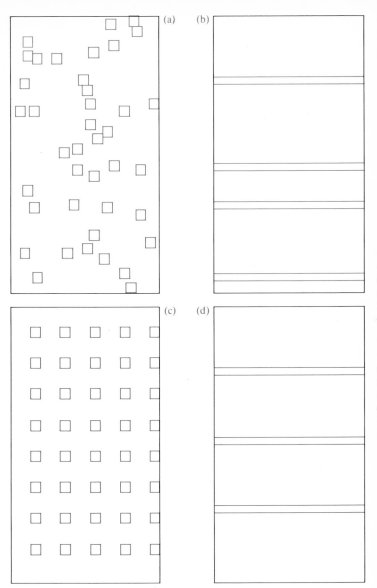

Different strategies for surveying an area by probability SAMPLING; *in each case a 10% sample is taken.* a. *Random quadrats.* b. *Random transects.* c. *Systematic quadrats.* d. *Systematic transects.*

closely the observations obtained from the part examined (the 'sample') represent the characteristics of the whole group being studied (the 'population'), by using fixed rules of random selection so that each unit is given a known chance of selection. The theory of probability sampling is well developed, but there are many problems in its application to archaeological data. One difficulty is that the object of archaeological interest (the 'target population') is the past human activity in the area, but the evidence available for study (the 'sampled population') is the area and its content of archaeological data. Probabilistic inference can be applied to estimating the nature of the sampled population, but the inference to the target population must be through the non-random formation processes that produced the archaeological record.

Techniques of random sampling are best developed in regional survey, where it is in many cases impossible to obtain complete coverage of an area. Several different sampling designs have been evolved, all using the principle of 'cluster sampling'; this is an indirect method of sampling, used where the population being studied is not itself available for sampling—in this case the sites in an area cannot be sampled because they are not known in advance. Instead, blocks of land containing the sites are sampled, giving a rather less secure estimate of the total population of sites. The sample units of land chosen are usually either squares ('quadrats') or long strips ('transects') of fixed size. They may each be located randomly ('simple random sampling'), or arranged in a regular pattern to ensure even coverage with only the starting point randomly chosen ('systematic sampling'). The area under study may be divided into sub-zones ('strata') such as river valley, coast, mountain, and each stratum can be sampled separately to give a more precise estimate of the whole population. The choice of sample design, the size of the sample units and the proportion of the population sampled (the 'sampling fraction') will all affect the result, but even with quite small fractions accurate estimates of the entire population of sites within an area can be obtained. The method is particularly good at estimating the number of different types of site within the area, though it may easily fail to locate even big or important sites if they are few in number; sampling may also fail to reveal details of the spatial organization of the sites.

Techniques for sampling within a single site are less well developed, though some of the problems are similar to those of regional sampling. The same types of sampling may be appropriate, though again estimates of the quantity of different features such as pits or houses will be given more easily than details of their organization. Methods are also being developed for the sampling of large groups of artefacts; excavations frequently produce very large quantities of bone or flint, and it has been shown that it is often necessary to study only a small sample of the whole population to obtain a reliable estimate of its character.

Ref.: MUELLER, J. W. *Sampling in Archaeology*. Tucson, Arizona, 1975.
CHERRY, J. F., GAMBLE, C., and SHENNAN, S. (eds.) *Sampling in Contemporary British Archaeology*. Oxford, 1978.

Scanning electron microscopy

A technique used to gain information on the microtopography of the surface of a wide range of materials from ceramics and metals to stone, teeth and hair. Its advantages over transmission electron microscopy (q.v.) include a greater depth of focus at high magnification, and its ability to deal with specimens of much greater bulk, so that it is less destructive. A high energy electron beam is passed through a series of magnetic lenses which demagnify the beam diameter; by means of sets of scanning coils the beam is deflected over the surface of the specimen. The backscattered electrons and secondary electrons emitted are detected by means of a scintillation or semiconductor counter. In both cases the angle at which the beam hits the surface of the specimen determines the number of backscattered and secondary electrons detected, and thus the pattern of contrast revealed represents the topography of the surface of the specimen. The chemical composition of the material of the surface can also be deduced from the backscattered electrons (beta-ray backscattering, q.v.).

Ref.: THORNTON, P. R. *Scanning Electron Microscopy.* London, 1968.

Scatter diagram

A method of presenting visually data which might otherwise be offered in purely numerical form. It consists of the plotting of units, as dots, against an x and a y axis representing two attributes, so that relationships between attributes as well as relationships between units may be shown. If clustering of dots into different groups occurs, it may suggest the presence of different classes; for example, a group of pots may be short and fat or tall and narrow, though basically of the same form, and clustering may simply suggest different potters. It is also possible to see whether one attribute co-varies with another, for example, whether all taller pots are

A SCATTER DIAGRAM *plotting two measurements of bovine radii from Troldebjerg, Denmark, showing the clear differentiation of two groups thought to represent male and female cattle (after* **Higham and Message 1969***).*

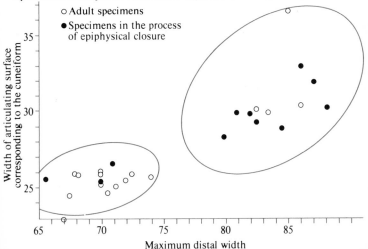

also thinner. This can be seen by the grouping of the dots around the line from bottom left to top right of the diagram.

Scorper

A metalworking tool with a broad sharp edge used for removing the background from designs on metalwork to allow the pattern to stand out. The tool may also be 'walked'—moved forward (or backward) through the metal on alternate corners—thus producing a zig-zag or tremolo line. It is likely that scorpers had to be of iron or steel to work on bronze, and therefore they may belong to later stages in the development of metalworking than tracers (q.v.).

Ref.: LOWERY, R. P., SAVAGE, R. D. A., and WILKINS, R. L. 'Scriber, graver, scorper, tracer: notes on experiments in bronzeworking technique', *Proc. Prehist. Soc.* 37 (1971), 167–82.

Scriber

A metalworking tool used for outlining designs on metalwork prior to chasing, engraving or repoussé work. Occasionally traces of this preliminary work can be seen where subsequent tooling has not completely obliterated it.

Seasonality of occupation

This term implies the exploitation of different environments at different times of the year by the same group of people. Transhumance (q.v.) is one instance of this practice, where high pastureland is grazed in the summer. Other instances are the exploitation of water resources for fish or waterbirds at the appropriate season when the area is not winter-flooded. The following of wild herds of, for example, deer, by hunter-gatherers also comes into this category, since such herds, and therefore the following groups, usually move back to their original starting place each year. If two sites within a given region but with different environments are occupied by the same group at different times, then population studies based on numbers of sites of a given phase must clearly take this seasonality of occupation into account.

Secondary working *see* RETOUCH

Section

In the context of an excavation this term defines a technique used for recovering the stratigraphy of a site or details of a particular feature. A baulk (q.v.) is left across a feature or a complex of features, or a hole is cut out of a feature and trimmed to a flat face in which layers and changes in soil colour may be examined. Two features such as ditches may run together: a section may show evidence of one cutting through another, therefore providing a sequence. Alternatively, a half-section of a pit (removing half the pit filling back to a diameter line) will show the method of filling (tipline, q.v.). Sections automatically occur when the grid method (q.v.) of excavation is used, on all four sides of each trench.

A SECTION *across two ditches at Portway East, Andover, Hampshire, England, showing clearly the right-hand ditch cutting across the filling of the left-hand one, thereby establishing the sequence.*

Sediment

A layer of soil or rock particles which are no longer in the place where they were formed geologically but which have been redeposited away from their source. The agencies of redeposition can be weathering and erosion, though man can also move such material around, creating archaeological sediments.

Sere

A developmental stage, one of a series, which forms part of the build-up towards a vegetational climax (q.v.). During the seres there are gradual changes in the ecosystem (q.v.): each sere may lack one or other of the dominant forms of the climax, but may contain new species which eventually make up the climax vegetation. Current theories suggest that the climax itself may not be much more stable than the seres.

Seriation

A process in which groups of archaeological material, such as assemblages of pottery or the grave goods deposited with burials, are arranged into chronological order. The types that comprise the assemblages to be ordered in this way must be from the same archaeological tradition, and from a single region or locality; this reduces the amount of variation in their contents that is due to social or geographical factors. It is also necessary to assume that the types used in the study have a potential chronological significance. The search for chronological order then rests on the observed fact that different types and styles of artefact or decoration come into and go out of fashion in a known way; this is described as lenticular, with a fast rate of adoption, a period of maximum use and then a long decline. When these patterns are displayed in the form of a bar chart (q.v.), they produce characteristic shapes known as 'battleship curves'. With a small number of groups and of component

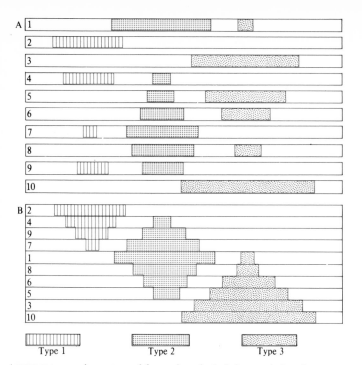

A SERIATION *graph constructed for ten hypothetical sites producing three pottery types in different frequencies.* a. *shows the unordered material;* b. *shows the material ordered into a relative chronological framework (*after *Knudson 1978).*

types, the data can be sorted by hand and eye to produce the best approximation to the expected pattern in a series of bar charts on paper. With larger numbers automatic processing by computer may be necessary, though a variety of quick methods have been suggested. The computer can be made to sort the data either in terms of the quantities present in the groups, or of the similarity between groups. Whatever method is used, the order produced is theoretically chronological, but will need archaeological assessment; in particular, the sequence could run in either direction, and some external evidence is needed to determine which end is the beginning and which the end.

Ref.: DORAN, J. E. and HODSON, F. R. *Mathematics and Computers in Archaeology.* London, 1975, 267–84.

Series

This term is used to describe a number of cultures or industries broadly related in time and space and yet discrete entities. The implication is one of some type of inter-group relationship, common ancestry, or similarity of interaction with the environment, though the term is in no way explicit.

Settlement pattern

The distribution of archaeological sites within a particular geographical area, which reflects the relationship of the inhabitants with their environment, and the relationship of groups with each other within that environment. Factors influencing the pattern of settlement in any area may include the subsistence strategy, the political structure, the social structure, population density and therefore carrying capacity. The analysis of settlement patterns by various means may produce results relating to all these questions.

Shadow mark *see* AERIAL PHOTOGRAPHY

Shifting cultivation *see* SLASH-AND-BURN AGRICULTURE

Sickle gloss

The gloss which occurs on the edge of flint sickle blades, and which is caused by the wear of the blade against the phytoliths (q.v.) in the grasses being reaped. The phytoliths occur in both wild and cultivated grasses, so that the presence of sickle gloss, indeed even the presence of a sickle, does not imply the practice of crop cultivation but simply grass collection of some kind.

Silhouette

The stain or shadow left in certain soils and under certain environmental

The SILHOUETTE *of a skeleton lying on its side under Tumulus II at Elp, Netherlands.*

conditions by organic or other objects whose substance has disappeared. The term has also been used to define any altered substance, for example woven cloth preserved by being close to a bronze or iron object whose corrosion products have changed the cloth into these metallic by-products. Silhouettes of timber, for example the shadow of a post in a post-hole, are relatively common. Skeletal remains are rarer but very useful where they occur. Where the soil is too acid to preserve the bone, the mineral component of bone may result in an iron manganese stain which frequently has the shape of a skeleton.

Site catchment analysis
A technique devised by E. Higgs and C. Vita-Finzi for 'the study of the

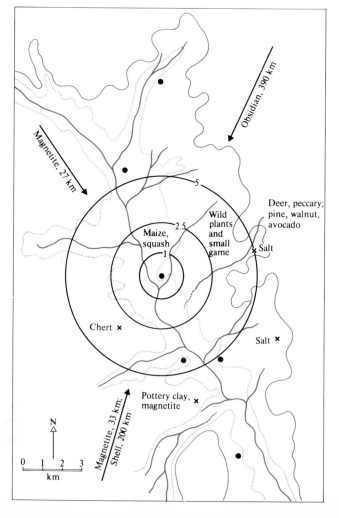

relationship between technology and those natural resources lying within economic range of individual sites'. It is an extension of the least-cost principle, and rests on the assumption that the further the resource area is from the site, the less likely will be its exploitation; beyond a certain point costs will be too great for exploitation to be economic. The catchment area is defined by drawing a circle around the site; the radius has often, and perhaps over-dogmatically, been set at 5km. (i.e. an hour's walk) for agriculturalists and 10km. (i.e. two hours' walk) for hunter-gatherers, figures which represent ethnographically observed averages. Within the catchment area the proportions of such resources as arable or pastoral land are calculated, and from these figures conclusions can be drawn concerning the nature and function of the site. There are many problems in using the technique: the radius measures geographical distance rather than walking time, which may vary considerably in different terrains; the cost of exploitation and the value of the resources are measured by modern criteria, not those perceived by the community; more specifically, a site could support itself by agriculture on a small fraction of a 5km. radius catchment area, so that a small proportion of arable land does not necessarily imply a non-agricultural economy. Nevertheless, the technique does offer a valuable and reasonably objective method for analysing relationships between site location, technology and available resources.

Ref.: VITA-FINZI, C. and HIGGS, E. S. 'Prehistoric economy in the Mount Carmel area of Palestine: site catchment analysis', *Proc. Prehist. Soc.* 36 (1970), 1–37.

Skeuomorph

An artefact, or part of an artefact, which represents in decorative form a feature which was originally functional. A purely decorative bow attached to a shoe is a skeuomorph of the laces once used to tie it; triangular shapes drawn below handles on pottery are skeuomorphs of the metal plates by which the handles on metal prototypes were attached. Frequently a

Left: SITE CATCHMENT ANALYSIS *An analysis of the north-east valley of Oaxaca, with site catchment circles of 1.0, 2.5 and 5.0 kms. radius centred on the village of San José Mogole, showing the availability of different local resources within each circle as well as materials brought in from further afield (after Flannery 1976).*

SKEUOMORPH: *A schist dish from a tomb at North Saqqara, Egypt, c. 2700 BC, showing a direct imitation of basketry in the decoration. 22.7 × 14 cm.*

skeuomorph may yield important information about vanished types, for example when organic materials like basketry are recorded in this way.

Slag

Slag is the glassy material made up of impurities which is removed from metal during smelting (q.v.). In the case of copper ores, the silicious material in the ore combines with such materials as potash or soda, producing a vitreous substance which is less dense than copper and thus floats on the surface. The silica in iron ores may not be so easily driven off, and a material containing a flux, such as lime, may be added during the smelting process in order to assist the formation of slag. It is not always easy, even with chemical analysis, to distinguish between slags of copper and iron smelting, and frequently slag is confused with cinder and other industrial products by archaeologists.

Slash-and-burn agriculture

This primitive form of agriculture is also known as swidden, shifting cultivation, roza and Brandwirtschaft. It is one of the earliest forms of cultivation, and consists of the clearance of small areas of forest by the burning and cutting down of trees and bushes, followed by the planting of crops in the clearance and their harvesting and replanting for a few years. As in other forms of primitive agriculture, without fertilizers the land soon loses its nutritional value, and the clearance must be left fallow, to grow over again, while more of the forest is cleared. A return to the original plot may be made after a reasonable length of time, hence shifting cultivation and cyclic agriculture (q.v.).

Sleeper beam

This is a component in a particular method of construction for a timber building where the uprights, instead of being set into postholes or gullies, are inserted into solid timber beams laid out on the ground surface or in a narrow trench. Though trenches of this kind are frequently located, clues to the presence of sleeper beams laid on the ground are rare, consisting invariably as they do of stains on the surface of the site.

Slip

A form of surface finishing applied to a pot which should not be confused with burnishing or glaze (q.v.). The finished but unfired pot is covered with a thin layer of slip, a mixture of clay and water, which gives the pot a smoother and often less porous finish. A slip can be coloured, for example with haematite, in order to enhance the artefact, though with it being a clay product, it is subject to the same colour variation through different firing conditions (oxidizing or reducing) as the clay itself. Haematite slips, intended to be red, occasionally fire to a shiny black finish in a reducing atmosphere (q.v.).

Slopewash

A type of sediment formed by soil and rubble being moved downhill. The deposit may be caused by solifluxion (q.v.) or by ploughwash (q.v.); the first is natural, the second anthropogenic. The resulting deposit is characterized by poor sorting of particle size as established by particle size analysis (q.v.). In extreme cases the remains of archaeological sites may be carried downhill with the soil, resulting in a false location and mixed material.

Small finds

A term used in excavation to define artefacts which can be picked up and transported, as opposed to features (q.v.). However, in different areas the term means different things: in the New World, all artefacts of this sort (pottery, stone, bone, metal, etc.) can be called small finds, while in Britain there can be a distinction between finds and small finds. On a site producing few artefacts, any find may be dealt with as a small find, while on a site producing large quantities of material, a small find will comprise something special, unusual or unclassifiable (for example, the main body of finds may comprise thousands of sherds of pottery and animal bones: a piece of metalwork or a grinding stone may be treated separately as a small find). This separate treatment entails individual bagging and recording, as well as planning with precision. This latter course is taken since small special finds may frequently be the most useful chronological markers of a phase of a site.

Smelting

This is a major process in metalworking, the one which produces the usable metal from the parent ores. For copper smelting, the two main divisions of ore-type require different treatment. The oxide ores can be fairly easily smelted, since the minerals will be reduced to metal simply with the admixture of carbon to the ore and their heating together to about 1,100°C. Sulphide ores must first be roasted in contact with air, which causes chemical changes allowing the resulting material to be treated like oxide ores. Iron from iron-bearing copper ores can also be extracted in this way. During the smelting process the liquid metal flows to the bottom of the furnace, and the slag (q.v.) floats on the top and can be removed. The smelting of iron ores is a more complex matter, since the iron does not melt at the smelting temperature (1,100°C); without adequate ore porosity, or with lumps of charcoal too large, or with too much oxygen, the process will fail. However, if these complexities are mastered, a spongy mass of metal will result from the smelting, while the silica which is the main impurity of iron ores will have been tapped off as slag. After smelting, copper can be cast and iron can be forged.

Soil conductivity meter

An instrument used in electromagnetic surveying (q.v.). It can be used for the detection of metal, but is also reasonably successful for the location of archaeological features. The instrument has a transmitter coil which is fed with a continuous sinusoidal current, and a receiver coil: they are mounted at right angles to each other at opposite ends of a horizontal bar about a metre long: this is to avoid the direct pick-up of the signal by the receiver. The instrument is designed to pick up differences in conductivity between features and the surrounding soil, i.e. the reverse of a resistivity meter, but in practice it appears to respond rather to the magnetic properties of the soil. At present there are limitations on the instrument as a prospecting device, since only shallow features can be located; resistivity surveying (q.v.) is still more sensitive and versatile.

Ref.: TITE, M. S. and MULLINS, C. 'Electromagnetic prospecting on archaeological sites using a soil conductivity meter', *Archaeometry* 12 (1970), 97–104.

Soil mark *see* AERIAL PHOTOGRAPHY

Soil profile
The sequence of horizons in the soil which occur not as the result of stratification but as a result of weathering and other processes. The soil profile is made up of some or all of the following: the A or humus horizon, the E or leached horizon, the B or (B) horizons of accumulation or chemical weathering, and the C horizon of parent material. Different soil profiles occur in different environmental regions, ranging from rendsinas, through brownearths, to podsols, gleys and chernozems. The soil profile and the type of vegetation are interdependent, and man's activities have an effect on and are affected by both, so that soil analysis is important in archaeology.

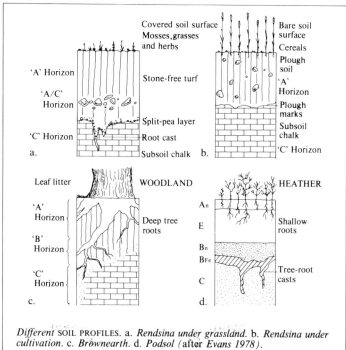

Different SOIL PROFILES. a. *Rendsina under grassland.* b. *Rendsina under cultivation.* c. *Brownearth.* d. *Podsol (after Evans 1978).*

Solifluxion

A term used to describe the slippage of soil and rock particles due to the freezing and subsequent thawing of the earth. Many of the deposits of intrusive accumulated soil in valleys and on the lower part of hills are due to the land having been glaciated, with the top level thawing in the spring and the water, unable to permeate the still-frozen subsoil, flowing downhill, taking with it chunks of loose material. Full glaciation is not necessary to cause solifluxion; hard winters with frozen earth and occasional thaws can cause minor solifluxion that may add to the accumulation of material. One important feature of solifluxion in archaeological contexts is that artefactual material may be moved from one deposit to another, for example from high on a hillside to the bottom. It is possible, too, that whole areas of archaeological sites may be covered with solifluxion material.

Sondage

A word used in excavation (Fr. *sonder*: to sound or investigate) to describe a usually small test-hole dug to establish the nature of a site or the depth of stratigraphy in different areas. A number of sondages may be dug so that the maximum of preliminary information may be gained with the minimum of effort and disturbance. In modern archaeology, this technique of pre-examination of a site is generally replaced by physical methods (e.g. magnetometer survey, resistivity survey, q.v.), or, if applicable, aerial photography, though a more sophisticated version of the technique of sondage digging would be classified as sampling (q.v.).

Spatial analysis

The systematic study of spatial patterning in archaeological data. The distribution map showing artefacts or sites has been in use for a long time in archaeology, but there are now rigorous mathematical and statistical techniques for examining such maps. Most of these techniques have been adapted from modern geography, such as locational analysis (q.v.) for the study of settlement patterns, and the use of distance-decay functions (q.v.), linear regression analysis (q.v.) and trend-surface analysis (q.v.) for exploring the distribution of artefacts.

Ref.: HODDER, I. and ORTON, C. *Spatial Analysis in Archaeology.* Cambridge, 1976.

Specific gravity determination

The measurement of the specific gravity of a metal artefact can be a useful non-destructive method of determining its composition, provided that certain criteria are fulfilled beforehand. The specimen should be a simple alloy of two metals, since more than that requires the identification of the extra metal(s) by other means, thus negating the simplicity of the method. The technique is generally used for coins where one part of the alloy may be gold; a comparison of the specific gravity of a gold alloy coin with pure gold allows the estimation of the concentration of the other metal, which should be silver or copper with known specific gravities. The actual procedure is quite simple: specific gravity is the ratio of the density of the material to the density of water, so the specimen must be weighed in the air and then suspended in a suitable liquid with a known specific gravity; the result is determined by an equation. Since the presence of a third metal in small amounts upsets the accuracy of the technique, the amount of fore-knowledge required is greater than in most of the other methods of determining the chemical composition of objects, and thus the use of this particular technique is limited.

Ref.: HUGHES, M. J. and ODDY, W. A. 'A reappraisal of the specific gravity method for the analysis of gold alloys', *Archaeometry* 12 (1970), 1–12.

Speculum
An alloy of copper and tin containing more than 30% tin. Ordinary bronze is composed of approximately 90% copper and 10% tin, and tends to be softer than speculum, which is hard and brittle due to the formation of intermetallic compounds. Speculum had a principal use in antiquity for certain coins amongst the Celtic tribes of central and western Europe.

Spelt
A species of wheat which was apparently not cultivated on the earliest of farming sites, but which appears only in the second millennium BC (*see* palaeoethnobotany). It is a hulled grain (i.e. grains and glumes do not separate during threshing), and was probably used for bread-making, porridge and even brewing.

Standard deviation
A term which describes the natural statistical distribution of a series of measurements around a mean value. It is most commonly encountered in archaeology in association with chronometric dating techniques like radiocarbon dating (q.v.), where each measurement is a calculation of date for the sample, and the final date given (for example, 2,400 ± 200) is a statistical description of a 'real' date. The standard deviation (±) as quoted means that there is a 66% chance of the real date lying within that range (for the above example, between 2,600 and 2,200); for greater probability, the date must be taken to two standard deviations (there is a 95% certainty that the date lies between 2,800 and 2,000). A single date with such a relatively large error is generally of less use than a series of dates from the same context, which may show a clustering around a central date.

State
A form of social organization characterized by the existence of a central government which is formally instituted and permanently effective. The actual positions within this government may be filled by a person or persons determined by a variety of selection procedures, but the institutional authority dominates all other organizations within the society.

It is the only body which can legitimately exercise force or violence within the society, and wields sufficient power to enforce its decisions, to coerce individuals and to exact payment from them. States are frequently marked, therefore, by the possession of an armed force for exaction and coercion, and a bureaucracy for record-keeping. A distinction can be drawn between primary states, those whose origin is independent of any contact with previously existing states, and secondary states, which arise from influences emanating from already established states.

Status
The position occupied by an individual in relation to all other members of the society. This may be determined by his personal achievements in life (achieved) or by his birth and ancestry (ascribed).

Stratigraphy
Although the term comes from geology, the theory of stratigraphy is a basic tool in archaeology without which chronologies and sequences of events could not be constructed. The theory is based on the observation that deposits laid down first will lie below those laid down later, and that in looking at a section (q.v.), the top layers are later than the bottom unless there are later intrusions into earlier deposits. An artefact found in the second layer down will date later (more recently) than one found in the seventh layer down, though the actual time difference will not necessarily be clear from the stratigraphy alone. Features which have been cut later into earlier layers should be visible by the differences in filling and the discontinuity in earlier layers. Objects found at the bottom of a late posthole will not be contemporary with artefacts found in a layer at a similar level which is in its original stratigraphical position. There can be problems where a feature filled with one type of material cuts into layers of the same material. Unless the later feature is recognized, objects of two different phases may appear to be stratified together. Minute differences in

STRATIGRAPHY *An example of how false conclusions can be drawn from a site if stratification is ignored or misunderstood (*after *Wheeler 1954)*

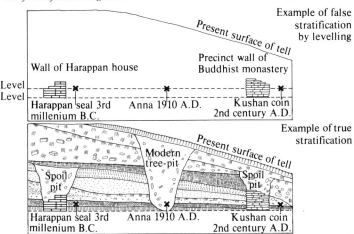

Example of false stratification by levelling

Present surface of tell

Wall of Harappan house

Precinct wall of Buddhist monastery

Level
Level

Harappan seal 3rd millenium B.C. | Anna 1910 A.D. | Kushan coin 2nd century A.D.

Example of true stratification

Present surface of tell

Modern tree-pit

Spoil pit | Spoil pit

Harappan seal 3rd millenium B.C. | Anna 1910 A.D. | Kushan coin 2nd century A.D.

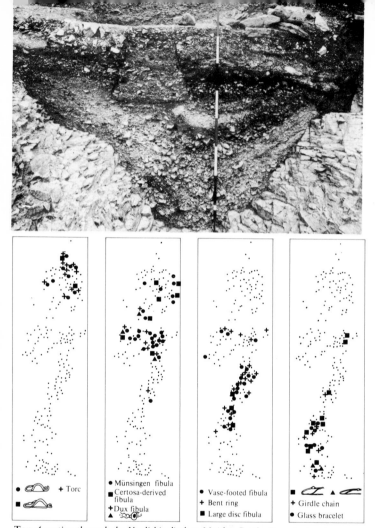

Top *A section through the Neolithic ditch at Maiden Castle, Dorset, showing a stratigraphically later feature dug into the upper layers.* Above *An example of horizontal stratification from Münsingen, Switzerland, where, in general, the later the grave in this Iron Age cemetery, the further it is from the starting point* (after *Hodson 1964*).

colour, texture and even smell may be all that tell the archaeologist of a change. As well as stratigraphy in the vertical sense, the superposition of layers, there is also a theory of horizontal stratigraphy, which works on the assumption that certain types of site, such as cemeteries, may grow outwards in one or more directions from a nodal point. Thus there would be a relative sequence from graves near the starting point to graves further away, and this has been seen to work on some sites. However, even in the best-known examples there are later graves placed among the early ones, and a stratigraphical sequence based solely on the placing of graves could clearly be fraught with errors.

Stray find

An object of some kind—pottery, metalwork, a coin, etc.—which has not been found in an archaeological context. Such finds may eventually be known to come from a site if subsequent examination shows a site in the region of the find, but even then it would not be stratified. Stray finds are useful if the total distribution of a particular type of object is required, but the absence of associated material or structures makes their interpretation difficult.

Striking platform

The part of a flint core which is struck to remove a flake or blade. It is normally a flattish area, preferably projecting, and is struck near the edge so that a flake is detached, leaving another suitable platform for a further blow.

Subsistence economy

The way in which a society exploits its environment to procure the means of feeding itself. Basically there are only two broad types of subsistence: exploitation of wild or of domesticated plants and animals, though there are very great variations within these two categories, and both may be practised in combination by a society. The term can also be used to describe the economic level of those who produce only enough food for their own consumption, without any surplus for other purposes.

Surface enrichment

A phenomenon which occurs mainly in a metal alloy coinage, where the more 'noble' metal in the alloy has a higher observed concentration at the surface of the coin than at the centre. A silver/copper alloy has a higher concentration of silver, a gold/silver alloy a higher concentration of gold. The reasons for this may be connected with the oxidation or corrosion of the less stable elements, or 'diffusion' effects, though the process is not fully understood. Since the composition of coins can be an important aspect of locating their source and, more generally, of understanding economic and historical events, any form of analysis which cannot take account of surface enrichment is clearly not applicable for coins. If the coin is not to be damaged by the taking of a sample, then neutron activation analysis (q.v.) is suitable.

Ref.: HALL, E. T. 'Surface enrichment of buried metals', *Archaeometry* 4 (1961), 62–6.

Swidden *see* SLASH-AND-BURN AGRICULTURE

Temper

A term used by archaeologists to describe material added to clay for

Sherds of Anglo-Saxon pottery from Sutton Courtenay, Oxfordshire, England, with holes remaining from burnt-out grass-tempering.

pottery making to reduce plasticity, which would otherwise cause shrinkage on firing. This filler material may be inorganic or organic: sand and ground flint are common, calcite and grog (q.v.), as well as shell and grass. In the case of the last-named, the firing process usually burns out the material, and only the marks left by its original presence remain.

Tempering
This is one of the processes in the manufacture of steel. Steel can be hardened by heating it to above $750°C$ in a reducing atmosphere and then by quenching (q.v.). Hardened steel thus obtained is, however, very brittle, a problem which can be at least partly resolved by tempering. This process consists of reheating to a lower temperature, around $450°C$, and then quenching at one of several points depending on the use to which the steel will be put.

Tephrochronology
A technique for the relative dating of horizons in volcanic regions by the mineralogical identification of different ash layers. Occasionally they can be tied in to absolute chronology where radiocarbon dates can be obtained from material contemporary with the deposit.

Terminus ante quem
(*Lat.* 'time before which'). This term defines a relative chronological date extracted normally from a sequence gained through stratigraphy. If a deposit can be securely dated by material found in it —for example, by a series of coins dating to the third century AD—then that deposit gives a *terminus ante quem* of the third century AD to a deposit proven to be stratigraphically earlier. In exceptional circumstances such a 'date' may be combined with a *terminus post quem* (q.v.) from an earlier phase to produce a date range for the intervening deposit.

Terminus post quem
(*Lat.* 'time after which). This term defines a relative chronological date given by dated material earlier than the deposit which needs dating. If a deposit contains dateable coins or pottery, then deposits stratigraphically later must be of a later date than that given by such material: the dated layer gives a *terminus post quem* for the undated deposit. If combined with

a *terminus ante quem* (q.v.), the deposit may be dated securely between the two.

Tessellated
A floor or other surface decorated with tesserae (q.v.).

Tessera
A small square of stone, coloured glass or tile, used with others to make mosaic patterns on floors, walls and ceilings.

Theodolite
An instrument used in surveying for measuring horizontal and vertical angles. It is used in archaeology for the surveying of sites, the accurate plotting of excavation trenches, in certain cases for the planning of features, and it can also be used in place of a level (q.v.) for determining heights and contours. There are different types of theodolite, though all include the telescopic sighting tube and horizontal and vertical scales for the reading of angles. The direction theodolite is normally called a theodolite, while the repeating theodolite is also called an American transit and tends to be used more in the New World. The first measures a 5 ′ arc, and is more accurate over a single measurement, while the second can only measure a 20 ′ arc and is less accurate over a single measurement, though as the name implies it repeats the measurements and can eventually be as accurate as the direction theodolite. Vertical readings are easier to take on the theodolite than on the transit as the levelling procedure is time-consuming on the latter, but is independent on the former because an optical device governed by a pendulum makes levelling automatic.

Thermal analysis
This comprises a group of techniques which are generally used to obtain information on the firing temperatures of pottery and other clay objects. The techniques involve the heating of the specimen under controlled conditions, usually up to 1,000°C, which causes changes indicating the presence of particular minerals. Differential thermal analysis requires the heating of a powdered sample of pottery simultaneously with the same amount of an inert substance: measurement of the difference in temperature between the samples allows the recognition of changes in, for example, heat absorption, which in turn can indicate the temperature at which the pot was originally fired. Thermogravimetric analysis, the study of the weight loss in pottery at certain points during heating to 1,000°C, can also pinpoint low firing temperatures. Thermal expansion measurements are based on the assumption that clay shrinks when fired. Heating in the laboratory causes expansion, but when heating continues above the original firing temperature expansion changes to contraction, and the pinpointing of the temperature at which this occurs should suggest the original firing temperature.

Ref.: TITE, M. S. 'Determination of the firing temperature of ancient

ceramics by measurement of thermal expansion: a reassessment',
Archaeometry 11 (1969), 131–43.

Thermoluminescence dating

A chronometric dating technique for the dating of pottery and other fired
clay artefacts. It is based on the principle that ceramic material, like other
crystalline non-conducting solids, contains small amounts of radioactive
impurities such as potassium, uranium and thorium, which emit alpha
and beta particles and gamma rays causing ionizing radiation. This
produces electrons and other charge-carriers, or holes, which become
caught in the traps or defects always present in the crystal lattice. Heating
of the pottery causes the electrons and holes to be released from the traps,
and they recombine with a release of the stored energy in the form of light,
or thermoluminescence (TL). The greater the number of trapped electrons, the more intense the TL; since this is held to increase with time, age
determination can result from measurement of the TL. There are several
factors to be borne in mind in the consideration of the technique. The
radiation comes from three main sources: internal radiation from the
sample (alpha and beta); gamma radiation from the soil; and cosmic
radiation. These affect different parts of the sample, for pottery is usually a
mixture of a fine grain matrix with mineral inclusions. The latter produce
the majority of the TL, while the matrix contains the impurities of
uranium and thorium which produce the alpha particles which form the
major part of the radiation dose. The inclusions and the fine grain must
therefore be measured separately (inclusion dating and fine-grain dating).
As well as the measurement of the natural TL, tests must be made on the
sample to ascertain its sensitivity to ionizing radiation; this is done by
artificially inducing radiation. In addition, the annual radiation dose
received by the sample is calculated by measurement of the uranium and

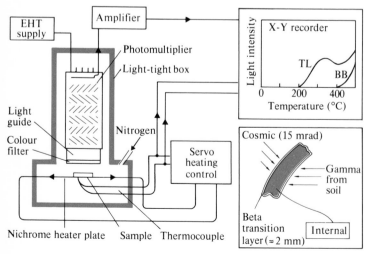

THERMOLUMINESCENCE DATING Opposite *A diagram of the equipment used for thermoluminescence measurements; and the annual radiation dose received by a potsherd, which allows the measurement of thermoluminescence (after Tite 1972). The 'Tang' Chinese horse, above, was shown to be a fake by thermoluminescence measurement.*

thorium in the sample (by counting alpha particles with a scintillation counter), measurement of the potassium (by flame photometry), and of the gamma ray dose from the soil where the pot was found. It is useful therefore to decide on samples for dating during excavations. Accuracy for the technique is generally claimed at ±10%, and results compared with radiocarbon dates are encouraging. It is a complicated technique, but it is being increasingly used for authenticity testing, and thus will presumably become more easily available.

Ref.: AITKEN, M. J., ZIMMERMAN, D. W., and FLEMING, S. J. 'Thermoluminescent dating of pottery', *Nature* 219 (1968), 442–5.

Thermoremanent magnetism *see* MAGNETIC DATING; MAGNETIC SURVEYING

Thiessen polygons

Polygons constructed on a map around a series of centres by drawing perpendicular lines at the mid-points between each centre and all its neighbours; they thus enclose the area nearer to one centre than to any other. The method is useful for defining theoretical territories related to each centre; they could be the areas served by a production or market centre, for example, or the region from which a centre draws its resources. These theoretical territories can then be tested by comparison with the actual archaeological data such as artefact distributions. The method

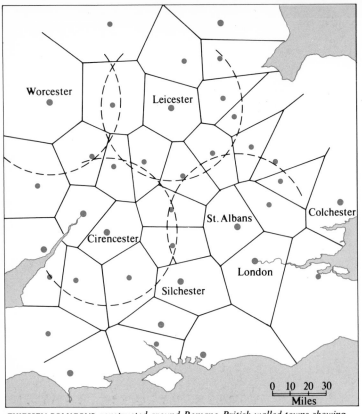

THIESSEN POLYGONS *constructed around Romano-British walled towns showing their notional territories; the smaller towns are spaced evenly from the higher order central places marked by the large circles (after Hodder and Hassall 1971).*

assumes that all the chosen centres are contemporary and of the same status, assumptions which are not always easy to confirm archaeologically. One restriction of the technique is that the resulting polygons give equal weight to all centres, whatever their size, although a larger market, for instance, might serve a larger area. In such a case it is possible to weight the polygons by drawing the lines not at the mid-point but at a point between one centre and its neighbour in proportion to their relative sizes, thus giving the larger centre a larger territory.

Ref.: HODDER, I., and ORTON, C. *Spatial Analysis in Archaeology.* Cambridge, 1976, 59–60.

Thin sectioning

The removal of a thin slice of material from an object, typically pottery or stone, for the purpose of examination under the petrological microscope (q.v.).

Tipline

This term is applied to a feature seen in excavation. In places on a site where rubbish material has been dumped, such as in pits and ditches or on mounds, the deposit assumes a sloping line as a result of the material slipping until it reaches a point of rest. Careful excavation can show the point from which the rubbish was deposited, and subsequent tiplines may allow conclusions to be drawn about the way in which the feature was filled or built up.

Topogenous peat

The type of peat which forms in low-lying areas like basins and infilled lakes, and which derives the majority of its moisture from ground water. The vegetation, more varied than that of blanket peat (q.v.), requires the calcium from the ground water, though the acid-tolerant *Sphagnum* moss may grow in the upper levels where rain provides most of the moisture. As with blanket peat, remains of man's activity may be preserved in topogenous peat formations.

Trace elements

The elements present in a mineral in minute proportions which are frequently characteristic of the original source of the material. Trace elements are not added deliberately to a substance, like minor constituents in an alloy, but occur naturally in the raw material. Quantitative analyses of substances like metal, clay and obsidian, carried out by methods like optical emission spectrometry (q.v.), and X-ray fluorescent spectrometry (q.v.) can show the amounts of these trace elements present and perhaps suggest a known source.

Tracer

A metalworking tool in the form of a small chisel which is hammered into the metal to give a short indented line. A tracer was frequently used to outline the raised areas on the surface of repoussé (q.v.) metalwork. Since hardness and sharpness are not necessary for chasing, a bronze tracer may be used to decorate bronze metalwork, and therefore tracers may have been used in the early stages of metalworking. Since a tracer is hammered, it cannot be 'rocked', so that the description of decoration as 'rocked tracer' is mistaken (graver, scorper, q.v.).

Ref.: LOWERY, R. P., SAVAGE, R. D. A., and WILKINS, R. L. 'Scriber, graver, scorper, tracer: notes on experiments in bronzeworking technique', *Proc. Prehist. Soc.* 37 (1971), 167–82.

Tradition

This word is frequently used in the examination and classification of industries (q.v.) to describe a continuing development of style which retains elements of the original industry. In America, a tradition can also refer to a sequence of whole cultures which develop out of each other. The term can cause problems in its usage: where an industry is described as belonging to one culture with the tradition of another (for example,

Mousterian of Acheulian tradition when describing flint industries), it is very unclear as to what is implied about the relationship of the two industries. It is thus an imprecise term which is used to express technological relationships whose nature is not understood.

Trait

This term can be used for any individual artefact or aspect of man's culture. The traits of a particular culture may be certain monument or artefact types, or social or ritual practices. The word is also used by archaeologists to describe individual elements within a technology or art form.

Transhumance

A phenomenon which forms one aspect of seasonality of occupation (q.v.). It consists of the movement of the farmers and their herds and flocks away from the winter settlement to upland pasture in order to exploit the different environment available at different seasons of the year. Spring to autumn is spent on the grassy hill or mountainside, while wintering of the animals takes place at the main settlement where fodder has been collected. This movement of farmers results in the occupation of two sites at different times of the year by the same group of people, and must be accounted for in suitable areas where population studies based on site densities are undertaken.

Transit *see* THEODOLITE

Transmission electron microscopy

This technique can be used in the examination of metals, ceramics and stone in order to extract information on the internal microstructure of the specimen or on the surface microtopography. A high energy electronic beam is focussed through a condenser lens on to the specimen; the beam is transmitted through the sample, whose image is magnified by further lenses and is eventually projected on to a fluorescent screen beyond which is a photographic plate which records it. For direct study of a specimen to gain information on its internal structure, the sample must be exceedingly thin, or it is opaque to electrons. This is achieved either by grinding up the material of the sample and depositing it on to carbon film, or by preparing thin foils of metallic or non-metallic material by electropolishing or ion-thinning techniques. Electron diffraction effects and patterns are used in this study. The replication method involves the reproduction of the surface of the specimen in thin plastic or carbon film, and the enhancing of the topography by depositing a metal film on the surface from an oblique angle; the metal-covered facets transmit the electrons with less intensity, and the resulting contrast on the screen can be studied for detailed topography. It is possible by these methods to study in detail such things as the wear marks on stone tools, or the techniques of pottery making through examination of the surface.

Ref.: HEIDENRICH, R. D. *Fundamentals of Transmission Electron Microscopy.* New York, 1964.

Trend surface analysis

A method of producing a generalized map from observed data. It may be compared to drawing contours to give a continuous map of height, though, unlike height, the archaeological observations to be mapped are discontinuous and at isolated points and must therefore be used to give information over a wider area. This can be done either by averaging the values at a number of points to produce a general value or by a form of linear regression analysis which finds the 'contours' which best fit the

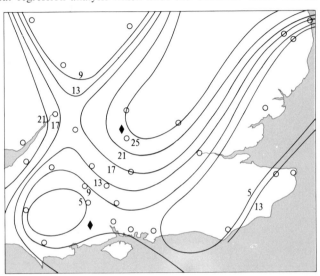

TREND SURFACE ANALYSIS *A trend surface analysis of the distribution of Oxford pottery products in the Romano-British period. It shows the concentrations around Oxford and the low contours around the New Forest where other pottery types are made and distributed (*after Hodder and Orton 1976*). Right Oxford and New Forest wares as analysed in the example.*

observations plotted on the map. The map thus produced shows a general trend of the distribution being studied, and can also show localized fluctuations, whether they are areas of greater concentration ('positive residuals') or of lower concentration ('negative residuals'). The technique is potentially a most useful one for displaying archaeological data in a simplified and generalized form in which it would be easier to examine the broad regional trends and the local variations and to explain them appropriately. It could be applied to many different artefact distributions at the regional level, and has also been used to describe the distribution of artefact types within a site, thus suggesting the location of structures and working areas.

Ref.: HODDER, I. and ORTON, C. *Spatial Analysis in Archaeology.* Cambridge, 1976, 155–74.

Trepanation

The practice of making a hole in a human head, while the subject is alive, by cutting out a piece of the skull. It is likely that this was carried out in antiquity, as it is today, as a form of surgery in attempts to cure tumours or to relieve the brain of pressure after injury. Its appearance has therefore much to say to those who study palaeopathology (q.v.), though it may also have been used in attempts to cure insanity. It is clear that many subjects survived the operation, for in several cases the bone has started to regenerate, while in others there is evidence for successive trepanations, in one case as many as seven.

TREPANATION *A trepanned skull and the removed disc from a Bronze Age tumulus on Crichel Down, Dorset, England.*

Triangulation

A technique used in the planning of archaeological sites before, during or after excavation. It can be used to plan features such as buildings, pits, ditches and postholes, or objects like significant finds whose exact position it is essential to record. It is one of the most accurate methods of planning, but since it requires two stages in the transference of the information in the field on to paper, it is not always the most suitable technique if large areas with complex features are to be planned at speed. The technique presupposes the existence of a permanent measured grid on the site marked by pegs, which is ultimately tied into the national grid. Tapes are run from the two nearest grid pegs to the object or feature to be planned, and the distance from each peg to the point being planned, the crossing point of the two tapes, is recorded. The transference of this information to the plan is accomplished by the location of the correct two grid pegs on the plan, the setting of a beam compass at the right distance (to scale) from first one peg and then the other, and the drawing of two arcs. The point at which the arcs cross represents the point at which the tapes crossed. A single point, like a small find, or a straightforward feature like a wall, where readings can be taken at intervals and joined up, are clearly easier to plan by this method than irregularly shaped features such as pits or narrow winding ditches, where so many points must be planned that the method becomes very time-consuming. In these cases, it may be easier to combine triangulation with grid-planning (q.v.), or to abandon triangulation altogether.

Tumbaga
An alloy of copper and gold used for making fine ornaments, particularly in the native cultures of Colombia, South America.

Tuyère
The nozzle which leads into a hearth, furnace or kiln from bellows. In antiquity it was usually of clay, and often survives as the only evidence for a metalworking site.

Typology
A technique used for the classification of objects based on their form and decoration. Groups of pottery, for example, may be created by placing together all those with long necks, all those with handles and all those with a pedestal base. Within these groups there may be different sub-groups based on variations in handle shape or decoration. Typology of this kind may be associated with chronology, in that it may be possible to place

The TYPOLOGY *of Iron Age (a–d) and early Roman (e,f) brooches.*

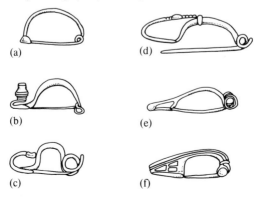

(a)

(d)

(b)

(e)

(c)

(f)

groups of the same kind of material in a sequence, though the direction in which the sequence is going is not always clear, since objects and decoration may become less or more complicated through time. A chronometric or stratigraphically produced relative date may help to order such a sequence. Typology on its own cannot be used as a dating technique, though it has been tried; as an aid to relative dating, it can be useful.

Uranium test

Like the fluorine test (q.v.), this method is used for the relative dating of bone, and is based on the same phenomenon. The calcium ions in the phosphatic mineral hydroxyapatite which bone contains are gradually altered during the time after burial into uranium ions as a result of uranium being in solution in the percolating groundwater. Thus the longer the bone has been in the ground, the more uranium will have been absorbed though, as for fluorine, the local environmental conditions affect the rate of alteration and therefore there is no universal rate which would yield absolute dates. The uranium is radioactive, and the measurement of beta particles emitted using a Geiger counter shows the amount present. The method is much less destructive than the chemical analyses required for the nitrogen (q.v.) and fluorine tests, but frequently all three tests are applied to the same material.

Ref.: OAKLEY, K. P. 'Analytical methods of dating bones', in *Science in Archaeology*. ed. D. Brothwell and E. Higgs. London, 1969, 35–45.

Varve dating

A technique for producing chronometric dates (q.v.) based on the annual formation of layers of sediment on lake and river beds in glacial regions. The material brought down by the glaciers is deposited in the lake during the annual melt, the heavier material first and the lighter later in the year. The annual layer is called a varve, and the changes in thickness every year, which occur through climatic variation, allow a sequence to be built up which can be recognized in other nearby deposits. The cross-linking of deposits allows the build-up of a long absolute chronology in calendar years, rather in the manner of dendrochronology (q.v.). Key sequences have been constructed in Scandinavia and in Minnesota, U.S.A. In neither case are the varves connected directly with archaeological deposits, though links may be made between varves and site through a comparison of pollen spectra or via obvious glacial deposits. Varve dating has a greater significance than just for local dating, since frequently there is enough organic material to allow radiocarbon dates to be calculated. There is therefore the possibility of using the calendrical varve chronology to calibrate radiocarbon dates, though results so far have shown the Scandinavian and Minnesotan sequences to disagree in their discrepancies with radiocarbon assays.

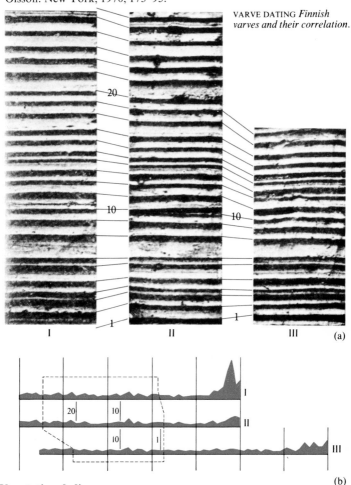

Ref.: TAUBER, H. 'The Scandinavian varve chronology and carbon-14 dating', in *Radiocarbon Variations and Absolute Chronology,* ed. I. U. Olsson. New York, 1970, 173–95.

VARVE DATING *Finnish varves and their correlation.*

(a)

(b)

Vegetational climax

A concept currently adhered to by many botanists and palaeobotanists which maintains that there are points in vegetational history beyond which there can be no progress until the environmental conditions change. The stages leading up to these climaxes (seres, q.v.) represent the gradual replacement of one ecosystem (q.v.) with another until a stabilized point is attained. In different areas these climaxes take different forms depending on climate: they may be tundra, mixed oak forest, evergreen forest, etc. A change in the climax vegetation therefore means a change in environmental conditions which may be naturally climatic or anthropogenic. Recent study of the faunal aspect of the system suggests that these climaxes may not be as stable as originally thought, and there remains much further research to be carried out.

Waster

As the name suggests, this is the waste product of the pottery manufacturing process. Occasionally, owing to bad choice of clays, mixing and wedging of clays, or malfunction of the firing process, a pot or batch of pots emerges distorted or split. The potter throws these useless pieces away, and if they are found during field survey they suggest the presence of kilns or other pot-firing structures.

Weed of cultivation

A plant which is unable to flourish in wooded shady areas but which finds its habitat in open regions such as fields associated with agriculture. With the removal of vegetational competition as a result of clearance of woodland, these weeds establish themselves, and it has become clear that where early agriculturalists cleared forest for the sowing of crops, these weeds appeared. It is now possible for palaeobotanists to recognize a phase of agriculture without direct evidence of cereals by noticing an increase in pollen diagrams of such weeds of cultivation as *plantago* (q.v.).

Wet sieving

A method of separating organic material (seeds, snails, insects, etc.) from its surrounding soil before drying, identification and analysis. It is a more time-consuming method of extraction than flotation (q.v.) by machine, but has the advantage of being more accurate in its results, since there is greater control over what is extracted from the sample. The sample is poured into a sieve in a bowl of water, the lumps of soil are broken up, and the organic material is trapped in the mesh while the soil particles sink.

X-ray diffraction analysis

A technique used to identify the major chemical components of an artefact, and also to extract information on the processes carried out during the manufacture of metalwork. For chemical identification, the method has been used mainly on pottery, though stone and metal corrosion products have also been analysed. For this technique a sample is taken from the artefact, is powdered and is submitted to a bombardment of X-rays with a sharply-defined wavelength. A characteristic powder diffraction pattern, a series of arcs, is reflected on to and recorded by photographic film; from these arcs, minerals present can be identified, and also, from the intensity of the darkening of the arcs, their concentrations estimated. The technique has certain limitations, such as the fact that certain substances are amorphous to X-rays and will not produce a diffraction pattern. For the examination of pottery, petrological examination is probably more accurate, and has the added advantage of giving much more information on the mineral grains themselves. X-ray diffraction can, however, yield information on the manufacturing processes of pottery; and it is used to obtain similar information from metal objects. For this purpose the back-reflection diffraction method is used: this is totally non-destructive, since the X-ray beam is directed straight on to the surface of the artefact, and the reflected rays are detected again on photographic film. The arcs can yield information on the structure of the metal, and from this the processes of manufacture can be inferred.

Ref.: TITE, M. S. *Methods of Physical Examination in Archaeology.* London, 1972, 285–8.

X-ray fluorescence spectrometry
This is a physical method of analysis which determines the chemical composition of substances such as pottery, obsidian and glass. Under most circumstances it is a totally non-destructive method of analysis, and therefore has this advantage over other physical methods (optical emission spectrometry, q.v.; atomic absorption spectrometry, q.v.). The specimen is subjected to irradiation by primary X-rays, releasing energy in the form of fluorescent X-rays. Since each element emits these secondary X-rays at characteristic wavelengths, an identification of the elements can be achieved through the determination of the wave-lengths, which are separated using a diffraction crystal. The concentration of each element may be estimated from the intensity of the X-rays. There are certain limitations to the use of this method of analysis. Because matter absorbs X-rays, only the thin surface layer of the object is analysed, which, though making the technique ideal for the examination of pottery glaze, presents problems with other substances such as metal whose surface may, through corrosion, have a different composition from the interior (surface enrichment, q.v.). In general terms the method is more suitable for the analysis of the major elements in a specimen, though trace elements can be determined in some cases. Certain required conditions for accurate measurement cannot always be met by archaeological artefacts which tend to be of various shapes and sizes. Errors may therefore occur, which can be corrected by the extraction and analysis of a sample from the material, though this naturally results in a small amount of destruction. Since automation of recording and sample changing is possible, large numbers of samples can be analysed at speed, which gives this method a definite advantage over atomic absorption spectrometry (q.v.) and optical emission spectrometry (q.v.).

Ref.: TITE, M. S. *Methods of Physical Examination in Archaeology.* London, 1972, 267–72.

X-ray microscopy *see* RADIOGRAPHY

X-ray milliprobe
This is a version of the X-ray fluorescence spectrometer (q.v.) which

satisfies the particular requirements of certain artefacts. The principle is the same as for X-ray fluorescence spectrometry; but in this piece of equipment the primary X-rays are collimated into a narrow beam which focusses on to a single point of the surface of the material under analysis. The secondary X-rays emitted from this point can be directed, by means of a curved diffracting crystal, straight to the detector. The spectrometer is outside the artefact, in contrast to standard X-ray spectrometry where the specimen is inside the spectrometer. The beam can therefore be directed to any point on the surface of an artefact, such as to a specific pigment on a picture or to a point on a coin cleaned of its surface layer (and thus its error-inducing corrosion), and yet cause no visible damage. The advantage that the X-ray milliprobe has over the electron probe microanalyser (q.v.) is the ease with which samples can be prepared.

Ref.: BANKS, M. and HALL, E. T. 'X-ray fluorescent analysis in archaeology: the milliprobe', *Archaeometry* 6 (1963), 31–6.

Sources for line drawings

ALCOCK, L. 'Excavations at South Cadbury Castle, 1967', *Antiquaries Journal* 48 (1968), 6–17.

BECK, C. W., WILBUR, E., MERET, S., KOSSOVE, M., and KERMANI, K. 'The Infrared spectra of amber and the identification of Baltic amber', *Archaeometry* 7 (1965), 96–109.

BORDES, F. *The Old Stone Age.* London, 1968.

BRIARD, J. *Les Depots Bretons et l'Age du Bronze Atlantique.* Rennes, 1965.

BROTHWELL, D. *Digging Up Bones.* London, 1963.

CATLING, H. W. and MILLETT, A. 'A study of the inscribed stirrup-jars from Thebes', *Archaeometry* 7 (1965), 3–85.

CORNWALL, I. 'Soil science and archaeology with illustrations from some British Bronze Age monuments', *Proceedings of the Prehistoric Society* 19 (1953), 129–47.

— *Soils for the Archaeologist.* London, 1958.

EVANS, J. G. *Land Snails in Archaeology.* London, 1972.

— *An Introduction to Environmental Archaeology.* London, 1978.

FAGAN, B. *In the Beginning: an Introduction to Archaeology.* Boston, Mass. 1972.

FLANNERY, K. V. (*ed.*) *The Early Mesoamerican Village.* New York, 1976.

GODWIN, H. *The History of the British Flora: a Factual Basis for Phytogeography.* 2nd ed. Cambridge, 1975.

HÄGERSTRAND, T. *Innovation diffusion as a spatial pattern* (translated by A. Pred). Chicago, 1967.

HANSEN, H. O. *Bognaeseksperiment.* Lejre, Denmark, 1966.

HIGHAM, C. and MESSAGE, M. 'An assessment of a prehistoric technique of bovine husbandry', in *Science in Archaeology* (*eds.* D. Brothwell and E. Higgs). 2nd ed. London, 1969, 315–30.

HODDER, I. 'Some new directions in the spatial analysis of archaeological data at the regional scale (macro)', in *Spatial Archaeology* (*ed.* D. L. Clarke). London, 1977, 223–51.

HODDER, I. and HASSALL, M. 'The non-random spacing of Romano-British walled towns', *Man* 6 (1971), 391–407.

HODDER, I. and ORTON, C. *Spatial Analysis in Archaeology.* Cambridge, 1976.

HODGES, H. *Technology in the Ancient World.* London, 1970.

HODSON, F. R. 'La Tène chronology, Continental and British', *Bulletin Institute of Archaeology London* 4 (1964), 123–41.

— 'Searching for structure within multivariate archaeological data', *World Archaeology* 1 (1), (1969), 90–105.

KNUDSON, S.J. *Culture in Retrospect*. Chicago, 1978.

LOBJOIS, G. 'La nécropole de Pernant (Aisne)', *Celticum* 18 (1969), 1–283.

MELLARS, P. 'Excavation and economic analysis of Mesolithic shell middens on the island of Oronsay (Inner Hebrides)', in *The Early Post-Glacial Settlement of Northern Europe* (*ed.* P. Mellars). London, 1978.

OAKLEY, K. P. *Man the Toolmaker*. London, 1972.

PEACOCK, D. P. S. 'Roman amphorae in pre-Roman Britain', in *The Iron Age and its Hill Forts* (*eds.* M. Jesson and D. Hill). Southampton, 1971, 161–88.

PIGGOTT, S. *Ancient Europe*. Edinburgh, 1965.

RENFREW, C. *Before Civilization: the Radiocarbon Revolution*. London, 1973.

RENFREW, C., DIXON, J. E., and CANN, J. R. 'Further Analysis of Near Eastern Obsidian', *Proceedings of the Prehistoric Society* 34 (1968), 319–31.

RENFREW, J., MONK, M., and MURPHY, P. *First Aid for Seeds*. (Rescue Publication No. 6) Hertford, England, n.d.

SAHLINS, M. *Tribesmen*. Englewood Cliffs, N.J. 1968.

SCHUMACHER, A. *Die Hallstattzeit im südlichen Hessen*. Bonn, 1972.

SEDDON, B. 'Late-glacial deposits at Llyn Dwythwch and Nant Ffrancon, Caernarvonshire', *Philosophical Transactions of the Royal Society* B244 (1962), 459–81.

SHACKLETON, N. 'Oxygen isotope analysis as a means of determining season of occupation of prehistoric midden sites', *Archaeometry* 15 (1973), 133–41.

SIEVEKING, G. DE G., CRADDOCK, P. T., HUGHES, M. J., BUSH, P., and FERGUSON, J. 'Characterization of prehistoric flint mine products', *Nature* 228 (1970), 251–54.

TITE, M. *Methods of Physical Examination in Archaeology*. London, 1972.

TRUMP, D. 'The Apennine culture of Italy', *Proceedings of the Prehistoric Society* 24 (1958), 165–200.

WEAVER, K. F. 'Magnetic clues help date the past', *National Geographic Magazine* 131 No. 5 (1967), 696–701.

WEBSTER, G. *Practical Archaeology*. 2nd. ed. London, 1971.

WHEELER, R. E. M. *Archaeology from the Earth*. Oxford, 1954.

WISSLER, C. *The American Indian: an Introduction to the Anthropology of the New World*. 3rd ed. Gloucester, Mass., 1957.

Further reading

General

BINFORD, L. R. and S. R. (*eds*) *New Perspectives in Archaeology*. Chicago, 1968.

CLARKE, D. L. (*ed.*) *Models in Archaeology*. London, 1972.

CLARKE, D. L. *Analytical Archaeology*. 2nd. ed. London, 1978.

COLES, J. M. *Field Archaeology in Britain*. London, 1972.

—*Archaeology by Experiment*. London, 1973.

HODGES, H. *Artifacts*. London, 1964.

— *Technology in the Ancient World*. London, 1970.

RENFREW, A. C. (*ed.*). *The Explanation of Culture Change: Models in Prehistory*. London, 1973.

SCHIFFER, M. B. *Behavioural Archaeology*. New York, 1976.

TRIGGER, B. G. *Beyond History: the Methods of Prehistory*. New York, 1968.

UCKO, P. J., TRINGHAM, R., and DIMBLEBY, G. (*eds.*) *Man, Settlement and Urbanism*. London, 1972.

WATSON, P. J., LEBLANC, S. A., and REDMAN, C. L. *Explanation in Archaeology: an Explicitly Scientific Approach*. New York, 1971.

Science and Dating

AITKEN, M. *Physics and Archaeology.* 2nd. ed. Oxford, 1974.

BROTHWELL, D. and HIGGS, E. (*eds*) *Science in Archaeology.* 2nd. ed. London, 1969.

FLEMING, S. *Dating in Archaeology.* London, 1976.

GOODYEAR, F. H. *Archaeological Site Science.* London, 1971.

MICHELS, J. W. *Dating Methods in Archaeology.* New York, 1973.

OLSSON, I. U. (*ed.*) *Radiocarbon Variations and Absolute Chronology, Proceedings of the 12th Nobel Symposium, Uppsala, Sweden.* Stockholm, 1970.

ROSENFELD, A. *The Inorganic Raw Materials of Antiquity.* London, 1965.

TITE, M. S. *Methods of Physical Examination in Archaeology.* London, 1973.

TYLECOTE, R. F. *Metallurgy in Archaeology.* London, 1962.

Environment

BUTZER, K. W. *Environment and Archaeology.* London, 1972.

CASTEEL, R. W. *Fish Remains in Archaeological and Palaeoenvironmental Studies.* London, 1976.

CHAPLIN, R. E. *The Study of Animal Bones from Archaeological Sites.* London, 1971.

CORNWALL, I. W. *Bones for the Archaeologist.* London, 1956.

— *Soils for the Archaeologist.* London, 1958.

DIMBLEBY, G. W. *Plants and Archaeology.* London, 1967.

EVANS, J. G. *Land Snails in Archaeology.* London, 1972.

— *An Introduction to Environmental Archaeology.* London, 1978.

LIMBREY, S. *Soil Science and Archaeology.* London, 1975.

MOORE, P. D. and WEBB, J. A. *Illustrated Guide to Pollen Analysis.* London, 1978.

RENFREW, J. M. *Palaeoethnobotany.* London, 1973.

SHACKLEY, M. *Archaeological Sediments: a Survey of Analytical Methods.* London, 1975.

UCKO, P. J. and DIMBLEBY, G. W. (*eds.*) *The Domestication and Exploitation of Plants and Animals.* London, 1969.

WELLS, C. *Bones, Bodies and Disease.* London, 1964.

ZEUNER, F. E. *A History of Domesticated Animals,* London, 1963.

Trade and Economy

EARLE, T. K. and ERICSON, J. E. *Exchange Systems in Prehistory.* New York, 1977.

HIGGS, E. S. (*ed.*) *Papers in Economic Prehistory.* Cambridge, 1972.

— *Palaeoeconomy.* Cambridge, 1975.

POLANYI, K., ARENSBERG, C. M., and PEARSON, H. W. (*eds.*) *Trade and Market in the Early Empires.* New York, 1957.

SABLOFF, J. A. and LAMBERG-KARLOVSKY, C. C. *Ancient Civilisation and Trade.* Albuquerque, 1976.

SAHLINS, M. D. *Stone Age Economics.* London, 1972.

Mathematics and Spatial Analysis

CHERRY, J., GAMBLE, C. G., and SHENNAN, S. J. (*eds.*) *Sampling in Contemporary British Archaeology.* Oxford, 1978.

CLARKE, D. L. (*ed.*) *Spatial Archaeology.* London, 1977.

DORAN, J. E. and HODSON, F. R. *Mathematics and Computers in Archaeology.* Edinburgh, 1975.

HODDER, I. (*ed.*) *Simulation Studies in Archaeology.* Cambridge, 1978.

HODDER, I. and ORTON, C. *Spatial Analysis in Archaeology.* Cambridge, 1976.

HODSON, F. R., KENDALL, D. G., and TARTU, P. (*eds.*) *Mathematics in the Archaeological and Historical Sciences.* Edinburgh, 1971.

MUELLER, J. W. (*ed.*) *Sampling in Archaeology.* Tucson, 1975.